EASY MICROSOFT EXCEL 2010

ISBN-13: 978-0-7897-4287-2
ISBN-10: 0-7897-4287-X

UK ISBN-13: 978-0-7897-4375-6
UK ISBN-10: 0-7897-4375-2

Library of Congress Cataloging-in-Publication Data is on file

Printed in the United States of America

First Printing: June 2010

TRADEMARKS

All terms mentioned in this book that are known to be trademarks or service marks have been appropriately capitalized. Que Publishing cannot attest to the accuracy of this information. Use of a term in this book should not be regarded as affecting the validity of any trademark or service mark.

WARNING AND DISCLAIMER

Every effort has been made to make this book as complete and as accurate as possible, but no warranty or fitness is implied. The information provided is on an "as is" basis. The author and the publisher shall have neither liability nor responsibility to any person or entity with respect to any loss or damages arising from the information contained in this book.

BULK SALES

Que Publishing offers excellent discounts on this book when ordered in quantity for bulk purchases or special sales. For more information, please contact

U.S. Corporate and Government Sales
1-800-382-3419
corpsales@pearsontechgroup.com

For sales outside of the U.S., please contact

International Sales
international@pearson.com

Associate Publisher
Greg Wiegand

Senior Acquisitions Editor
Loretta Yates

Development Editor
Todd Brakke

Managing Editor
Kristy Hart

Senior Project Editor
Lori Lyons

Copy Editor
Seth Kerney

Indexer
Lisa Stumpf

Proofreader
Dan Knott

Technical Editor
P.K.Hari Hara Subramanian

Publishing Coordinator
Cindy Teeters

Book Designer
Anne Jones

Compositor
Nonie Ratcliff

ABOUT THE AUTHOR

Mike Alexander is a Microsoft Certified Application Developer (MCAD) and author of several books on advanced business analysis with Microsoft Access and Excel. He has more than 15 years experience consulting and developing Office solutions. Michael has been named a Microsoft MVP for his ongoing contributions to the Excel community. In his spare time, he runs a free tutorial site, www.datapigtechnologies.com, where he shares basic Access and Excel tips to the Office community.

DEDICATION

For my family

ACKNOWLEDGMENTS

Thank you, Tim.

WE WANT TO HEAR FROM YOU!

As the reader of this book, *you* are our most important critic and commentator. We value your opinion and want to know what we're doing right, what we could do better, what areas you'd like to see us publish in, and any other words of wisdom you're willing to pass our way.

As an associate publisher for Que Publishing, I welcome your comments. You can email or write me directly to let me know what you did or didn't like about this book—as well as what we can do to make our books better.

Please note that I cannot help you with technical problems related to the topic of this book. We do have a User Services group, however, where I will forward specific technical questions related to the book.

When you write, please be sure to include this book's title and author as well as your name, email address, and phone number. I will carefully review your comments and share them with the author and editors who worked on the book.

Email: feedback@quepublishing.com

Mail: Greg Wiegand
            Associate Publisher
            Que Publishing
            800 East 96th Street
            Indianapolis, IN 46240 USA

READER SERVICES

Visit our website and register this book at quepublishing.com/register for convenient access to any updates, downloads, or errata that might be available for this book.

INTRODUCTION

Welcome to the world of Excel. Okay, that's a bit cheesy. But if you look around the business world, the financial world, the manufacturing world, and any other industry you can of, you will see people using Excel. Excel is everywhere. It is by far the most used program in the history of business applications. So in a very real way, it is truly a world of Excel. This is probably why you've picked up this book. You need a way to accelerate your learning and get up to speed in Excel.

Well, worry not, dear reader. Whether you're boning up on Excel for a new job (congratulations, by the way), a school project, or just for home use, this book is perfect for you. *Easy Microsoft Office Excel 2010* provides concise, visual, step-by-step instructions for the most common tasks you need to do in Excel. You won't be inundated with fancy descriptions of every little function and feature. We get right to the core tasks you need to get started fast. You learn how to create, edit, format, and print worksheets, as well as how to create charts and use Excel formulas. Just about everything you need to get up and running with Excel is in this one easy book.

WHAT'S IN THIS BOOK

First, you will explore the user interface. You'll get a sense of where to choose tasks, where to enter information, and how to move around in Excel. From there, you'll learn how to manage your Excel files. This includes creating new Excel workbooks, saving workbooks, and moving worksheets between workbooks.

Next, you'll explore the various methods for getting data into Excel. You will also walk through some techniques that allow you to manage and more easily work with the data in your Excel worksheets.

You'll continue on with the topic of formatting data. Here, you'll learn how to make your workbook your own by adding colors and applying fonts. You'll also learn how to make your data more readable by applying number formatting and cell formatting.

After you've covered the basics, you'll get a solid introduction to Excel functions and formulas. You'll first learn how to create and implement your own formulas. Then you'll get tutorials on how to use the most commonly used Excel functions.

Next, you'll explore charting in Excel. Here, you'll get an understanding of how to create charts in Excel and how to customize them to fit your needs. From there, you'll continue on to discover some of the ways you can add graphics and other visualizations into your Excel worksheets.

We'll round out your introduction to Excel with the topic of printing. Although printing sounds trivial, you'll discover that there are many print options you can use to configure your workbooks to print properly.

Finally, for those of you preparing yourself for a corporate job, Chapter 9, "Working with Excel Pivot Tables," introduces you to the topic of Pivot Tables. One of the most useful features in Excel, pivot tables allow any Excel analyst to analyze large amounts of data with just a few clicks.

After going through all the topics covered in this book, you will be able to say that you know how to use Excel!

Chapter 1

WORKING WITH THE EXCEL USER INTERFACE

THE RIBBON USER INTERFACE

For those of you who have worked with Microsoft Excel 2003, the first thing you will notice when using Microsoft Excel 2010 is that Microsoft has done away with the standard toolbar. That is, you don't see the typical pull-down menus found in older versions of Word, PowerPoint, and Excel. Instead, you'll see the interface dubbed the *Ribbon*.

The Ribbon was actually introduced with the Release of Office 2007 as a significant departure from the old way of selecting commands. Instead of having to drill into multiple levels of toolbars to find the command that you need, the Ribbon brings your favorite commands out into the open and even allows you to discover some new commands you never knew existed.

The Ribbon is made up of five basic components: the Quick Access Toolbar, tabs, groups, command buttons, and dialog launchers. The Quick Access Toolbar is essentially a customizable toolbar that allows you to add commands that are most important to your daily operations. Tabs contain groups of commands that are loosely related to core tasks. In fact, it helps to think of each tab as a theme. Groups contain sets of commands that fall under the umbrella of that tab's core task. Each group contains commands buttons, which are objects you click to select the action you want to execute. Dialog launchers are located in the lower-right corner of certain groups. Clicking on any one of these activates a dialog box containing the full spectrum of options for a given group.

THE ANATOMY OF THE RIBBON INTERFACE

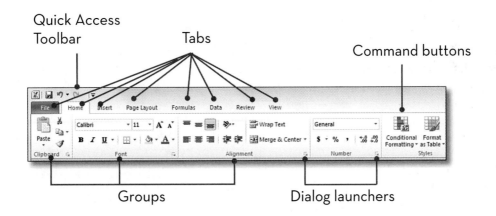

Quick Access Toolbar

Tabs

Command buttons

Groups

Dialog launchers

FAMILIARIZING YOURSELF WITH THE RIBBON TABS

Each tab in the Ribbon contains groups of commands that are loosely related to a central task. Don't be alarmed by the number of commands on each tab. As you go through this book, you'll quickly become familiar with each of the common Excel commands. For now, take some time to get familiar with each of Excel's default tabs.

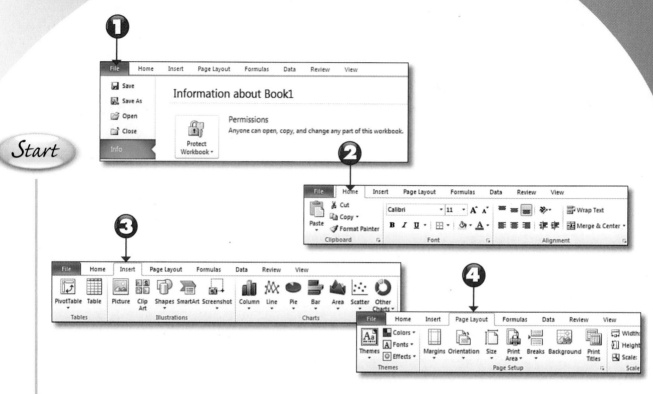

Start

1️⃣ Click the **File** tab. This tab contains all the higher-level Excel commands, such as open, save, print, and close.

2️⃣ Click the **Home** tab. This tab contains commands for common actions such as formatting, copying, pasting, inserting, and deleting columns and rows.

3️⃣ Click the **Insert** tab. This tab contains commands that allow you to insert objects such as charts and shapes into your spreadsheets.

4️⃣ Click the **Page Layout** tab. This tab holds all the commands that allow you to determine how your spreadsheet looks, both onscreen and when printed.

Continued

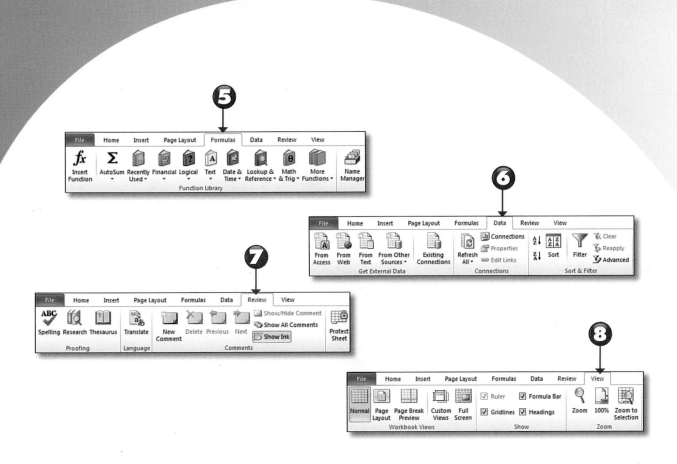

⑤ Click the **Formulas** tab. This tab holds all the commands that help define, control, and audit Excel formulas.

⑥ Click the **Data** tab. This tab features commands that allow you to connect to external data, as well as manage the data in your spreadsheet.

⑦ Click the **Review** tab. With commands such as Spell Check, Protect Sheet, Protect Workbook, and Track Changes, the theme of the Review tab is protecting data integrity in your spreadsheet.

⑧ Click the **View** tab. The commands on this tab are designed to help you control how you visually interact with your spreadsheet.

End

TIP

Minimizing the Ribbon If you feel the Ribbon takes up too much space at the top of your screen, you can minimize (hide) it. Right-click on the Ribbon and select Minimize the Ribbon. At this point, the Ribbon only becomes visible if you click on a tab. To revert back to the default Ribbon view, right-click the Ribbon and click Minimize the Ribbon again. ■

UNDERSTANDING CONTEXTUAL TABS

Contextual tabs are special types of tabs that appear only when a particular object is selected, such as a chart or a shape. These contextual tabs contain commands that are specific to whatever object has the current focus.

To see a contextual tab in action, add a shape to a spreadsheet. After a shape has been added, a new Format tab appears. This is not a standard tab, but a *contextual* tab—meaning it only activates when you are working with a shape.

You can follow the steps in this walkthrough to add a shape. Shapes and other graphics are covered in detail in Chapter 7, "Working with Graphics."

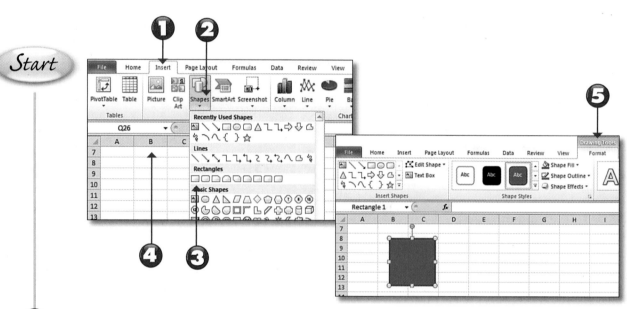

1 Click the **Insert** tab.

2 Click the **Shapes** command button.

3 Select the rectangle shape.

4 Click anywhere on your spreadsheet to embed your selected shape.

5 Click on your shape and note the Contextual tab that appears each time the shape is activated.

End

UNDERSTANDING WORKBOOKS AND WORKSHEETS

An Excel file, often referred to as a *workbook*, contains one or more spreadsheets, or *worksheets*. Each box in the worksheet area is referred to as a *cell*. Each cell has a *cell address*, which is comprised of a *column reference* and a *row reference*. The letters going across the top of the worksheet make up the column reference. The numbers going down the left side of the worksheet make up the row reference. For example, the address of the top, leftmost cell is A1. This is because the cell is located at the intersection of the A column and row 1.

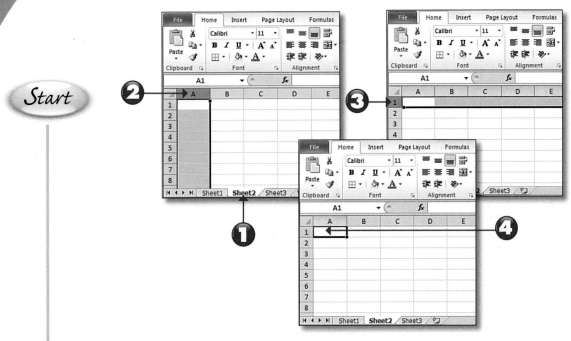

1. Click a worksheet's tab to view that worksheet's area.

2. Click the column reference and observe how the entire column is selected.

3. Click the row reference and observe how the entire row is selected.

4. Click the cell intersecting at column A and row 1. Notice how you can select a single cell on the worksheet area.

End

NOTE

The Big Grid Excel 2010 has 1,048,576 rows and 16,384 columns. This means that there are more than 17 billion cells in a single Excel worksheet. So what happens if you need more than a million rows and more than 16,000 columns? Well, the answer is that you'll have to start a new worksheet. ∎

CUSTOMIZING THE QUICK ACCESS TOOLBAR

By default, the Quick Access Toolbar contains three commands: Save, Undo, and Redo. If you click on the drop-down selection next to the Quick Access Toolbar, you'll see that these three commands are only three of eleven that are available as pre-built or built-in options. Placing a check next to any of the options that you see here automatically adds each option to the Quick Access Toolbar. So, clicking New adds the New command, and clicking Open adds the Open command. You can literally click each one of these and have all these pre-built options available to you in the Quick Access Toolbar.

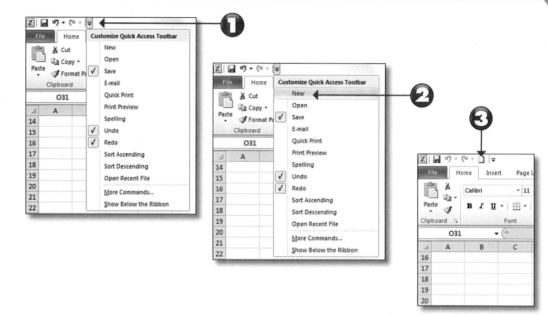

Start

1. Click the **Quick Access Toolbar** drop-down to see all the commands you can add.

2. Click the New pre-built command to add it to the Quick Access Toolbar.

3. Note that you now have a new icon on your Quick Access Toolbar.

End

NOTE

Moving the Quick Access Toolbar You can move the Quick Access Toolbar under the Ribbon by right-clicking its dropdown and selecting Show Below the Ribbon. ■

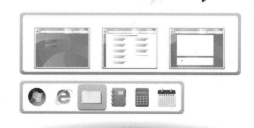

ADDING COMMANDS TO THE QUICK ACCESS TOOLBAR

You're not limited to the commands shown on the Quick Access Toolbar—you can add all kinds of commands. For example, if you often work with shapes, you can add the Shapes command to the Quick Access Toolbar.

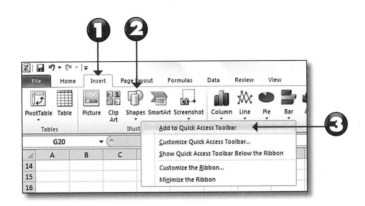

1 Click the **Insert** tab.

2 Right-click the **Shapes** command button.

3 Select **Add to Quick Access Toolbar**.

End

TIP

Adding Entire Groups You can add entire groups to your Quick Access Toolbar. For instance, if you often use the Illustrations group on the Insert tab, you can right-click on that entire group and click Add to Quick Access Toolbar. ■

ADDING HIDDEN COMMANDS TO THE QUICK ACCESS TOOLBAR

A closer look at the drop-down menu next to the Quick Access Toolbar reveals a command called More Commands. If you select this, the Excel options dialog box opens up with the Quick Access Toolbar panel activated. This panel allows you to select from the entire menu of Excel commands, adding them to your Quick Access Toolbar. This comes in handy if you want to add some of the more obscure Excel commands that aren't found in the Ribbon.

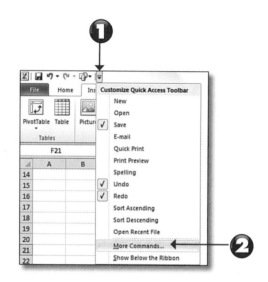

1 Click the **Quick Access Toolbar** drop-down.

2 Select the **More Commands** option.

Continued

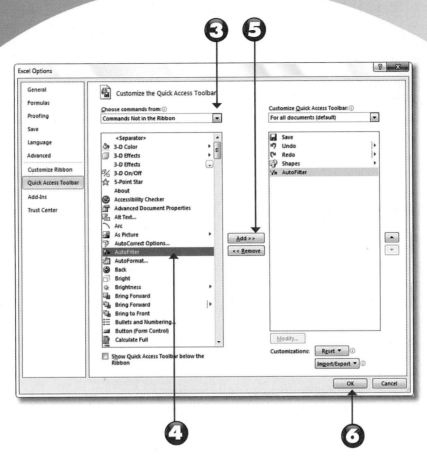

3 Choose **Commands Not in the Ribbon**.

4 Find and select the **AutoFilter** command.

5 Click the **Add** button.

6 Click the **OK** button to add the command to the Quick Access Toolbar.

End

TIP

Removing Commands To remove a command from the Quick Access Tool-bar, simply right-click on it and click Remove From Quick Access Toolbar. ■

Chapter 2

MANAGING WORKBOOKS AND WORKSHEETS

Some of the more fundamental tasks you'll undertake in Excel revolve around managing your workbooks and worksheets. A workbook is essentially a container that holds your worksheets. When someone refers to an Excel workbook, they are referring to the entire Excel file. A worksheet is the actual spreadsheet you work in. There can be many worksheets in a workbook—similar to pages in a book.

Excel 2010 includes a new File tab. This tab represents a return to the Excel 2003 look where you had a File menu option that wasn't a part of Excel 2007, which used a logo similar to the Start Menu icon in Windows Vista and 7. The logo in Excel 2007 caused confusion because most users did not realize it was a menu option. So Microsoft decided to reintroduce the File tab to the Ribbon interface.

The File tab exposes the Backstage view. In the Backstage view, you'll find every command you need to manage and work with Excel workbooks. The more common tasks found here are opening Excel workbooks, creating new workbooks, and saving workbooks. The Backstage view also provides options to share files, see file information, and access Excel application options.

EXCEL'S BACKSTAGE VIEW

Save a file

Save a file with a new name

Open an existing file

Close the current file

Get information on the current file

Get the list of recently opened files

Create a new workbook or worksheet

Set print options for the current file

Set Sharing options for the current file

Get Excel Help

Review and Edit Excel Application Options

Exit Excel

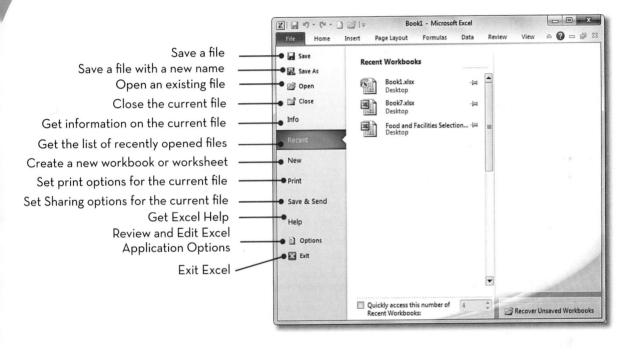

OPENING AN EXCEL WORKBOOK

Any time you want to work with an existing Excel workbook, you must open it first. The idea here is simple: You first tell Excel you want to open a file, and then select the file you want, using the Open dialog box.

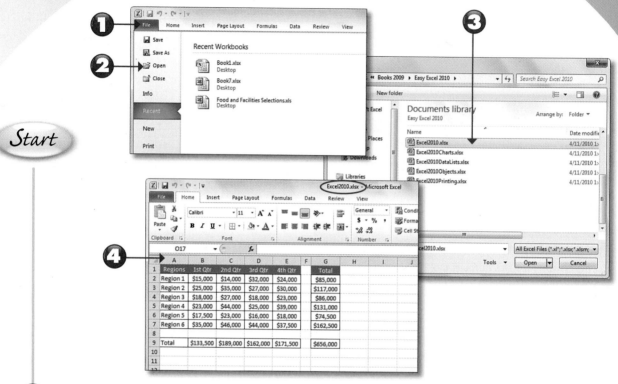

1 Click the **File** tab.

2 Click the **Open** command.

3 Use the Open dialog box to find the file you are trying to open, then double-click the file (or click the **Open** button).

4 Excel opens the workbook. Note the file name will be displayed at the top of the workbook.

End

NOTE

Creating a New Workbook   If you want to start a new workbook from scratch, you can click on the File tab and select New, then select Blank Workbook. Alternatively, you can go to your keyboard and type the shortcut key combination Ctrl+N. ∎

CLOSING AN EXCEL WORKBOOK

There may be instances when you want to close the current workbook but still remain working in Excel. In these situations, you'll find it handy to close only the current workbook. If you have been working in a workbook and try to close it, Excel asks you whether you want to save the workbook before it closes.

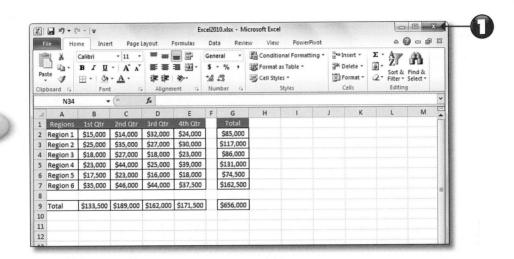

Start

Click the **Close** button (represented by the X) in the document window.

If you've made changes to the workbook, Excel prompts you to save your changes. Click **Yes** if you want to save any changes you have made, or click **No** if you do not. Excel responds accordingly, then closes the workbook.

End

SAVING A WORKBOOK

You should regularly save your workbooks as you work in them so you don't lose data. You can save a workbook as many times as you like, so saving often is a good habit to get into. You can also save your workbook under another name if you want to keep track of multiple versions of your workbook.

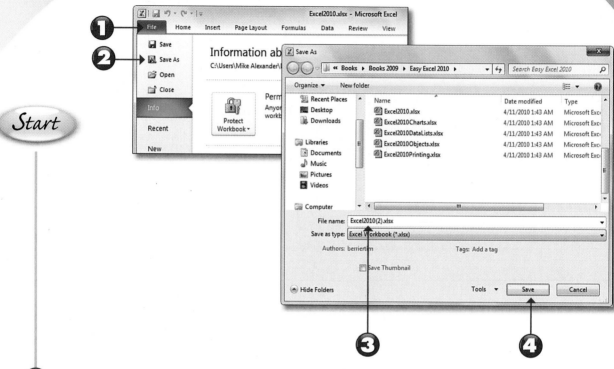

Start

1 Click the **File** tab.

2 Click the **Save As** command.

3 Use the Save As dialog box to locate the directory where you want to store your workbook and then enter the name for the file.

4 Click the **Save** button, and Excel saves your workbook.

End

NOTE

Clicking Save on the Quick Access Toolbar If you have already saved and named your file, you can resave it after making additional changes by clicking the Save command on the Quick Access Toolbar. Feel free to revisit Chapter 1, "Working with the Excel User Interface," to get a refresher on the Quick Access Toolbar. ■

SWITCHING BETWEEN OPEN WORKBOOKS

You can have multiple workbooks open at the same time and switch between them whenever you want. For example, you might be using two different workbooks to create one report. You can use the Windows Taskbar to quickly move from one workbook to another.

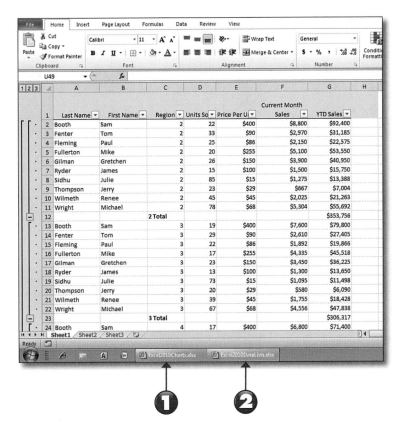

Start

1 With two or more workbooks already open, click the button on the Windows Taskbar that represents one of your open workbooks (in this case, the **Excel2010Charts.xlsx** button). This workbook becomes the active workbook.

2 Click a different workbook button on the Windows Taskbar (for instance, the **Excel2010DataLists.xlsx** button). This workbook becomes the active workbook.

End

NOTE

Using Alt+Tab to Toggle through Workbooks   You can also toggle through your open workbooks by using the Windows Alt+Tab toggle. With several workbooks open, you can go to your keyboard and type the shortcut key combination Alt+Tab. This allows you to cycle through all the open applications/workbooks and stop on the one you want. ■

SWITCHING BETWEEN WORKSHEETS

Similar to switching between multiple workbooks, you can switch between the separate worksheets within a single workbook. This allows you to review and edit data stored on separate worksheets within a single workbook.

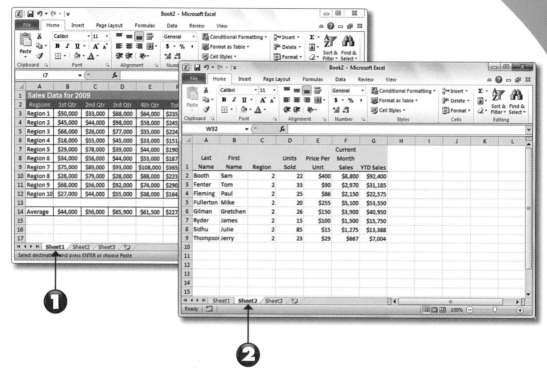

Start

 Click a worksheet tab (in this example, the **Sheet1** tab) to see the contents in that worksheet.

② Click a different worksheet tab (here, the **Sheet2** tab) to see the contents of that worksheet.

End

NOTE

Cycle through Sheets with the Keyboard   You can also cycle through the sheets in your workbook with your keyboard. Go to your keyboard and type the keyboard combination Ctrl+PgUp to go to the **next sheet**. Type the keyboard combination Ctrl+PgDown to go to the **previous sheet** . ∎

VIEWING MULTIPLE WORKBOOKS

Instead of constantly switching between workbooks, you can view multiple workbooks on-screen in Excel, and resize their windows as needed. This comes in pretty handy if you are comparing two or more workbooks, or working on multiple workbooks at the same time.

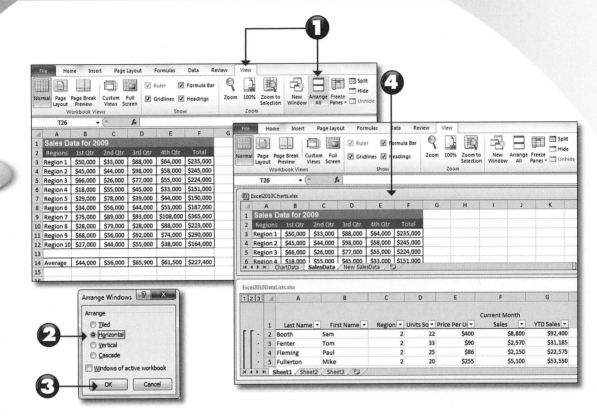

Start

1. Click the **View** tab and then select the **Arrange All** command.

2. Select how you want the windows arranged (for example, **Horizontal**).

3. Click the **OK** button.

4. Multiple workbooks are displayed simultaneously. Click on the title bar or in the body of the workbook you want to work in to make it the active worksheet.

End

NOTE

Vertical or Horizontal   If you need to compare two workbooks where the data is column oriented (data is mostly going up and down) use the Vertical option when arranging windows. If you need to compare two workbooks where the data is row oriented (data is mostly left to right) use the Horizontal option when arranging windows. ■

INSERTING AND DELETING WORKSHEETS

By default, Excel automatically provides you with three worksheets when a new workbook is created. As you work with Excel, you will likely find that you'll need to insert additional worksheets. Conversely, sometimes you'll need to delete ones you no longer use.

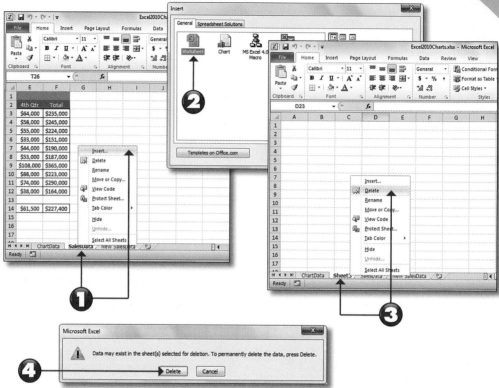

Start

1 Right-click on the worksheet tab before which you want a new worksheet placed, and then select **Insert**.

2 Double-click on the **Worksheet** icon. A new worksheet appears.

3 To delete a worksheet, right-click on the worksheet tab you want deleted and then select **Delete**.

4 Click the **Delete** button to confirm that you want the worksheet deleted.

End

NOTE

No Undo When Deleting Worksheets   Be careful when deleting worksheets, as there is no way to undo when deleting a worksheet. If you mistakenly delete a sheet, there is no way of getting it back. ■

RENAMING WORKSHEETS

You should always endeavor to use descriptive names for the worksheets in your Excel file. If you have a workbook that uses multiple worksheets, providing more descriptive names for your worksheets makes working within your workbook far easier than it would be if all your sheets were named Sheet1, Sheet2, and so on.

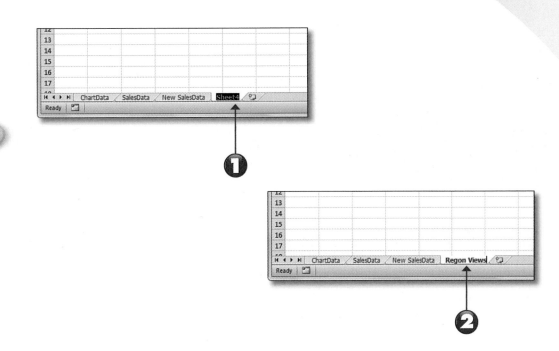

Start

1 Double-click the worksheet tab you want to rename. Alternatively, you can right-click the worksheet name and select **Rename**.

2 Type the new name and press the **Enter** key. Excel displays the new name on the worksheet tab.

End

NOTE

Worksheet Names Can't Be Too Long Excel has a 31-character limit on worksheet names. That is, your worksheets cannot have a name that exceeds 31 characters. ■

COLORING WORKSHEET TABS

As you add worksheets to your workbook, you will find an increasing need to organize your worksheets. To help with this, Excel allows you to color your worksheet tabs. If you want to indicate something specific about a worksheet tab—for example, if a worksheet contains preliminary data—you can assign it a tab color, such as red.

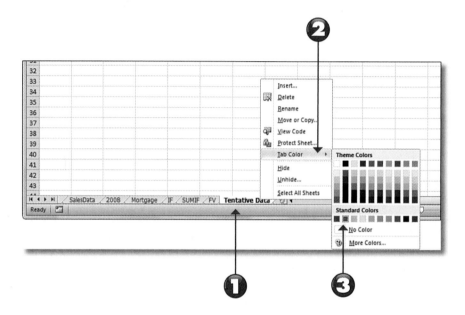

Start

1 Right-click on the worksheet tab you want to color.

2 Click the **Tab Color** menu option.

3 Select your preferred color. The color is immediately applied to your worksheet tab.

End

MOVING WORKSHEETS WITHIN A WORKBOOK

When Excel inserts a new worksheet, it always places it in front of the currently selected worksheet. You can, of course, move your worksheet tabs as you start organizing your workbook.

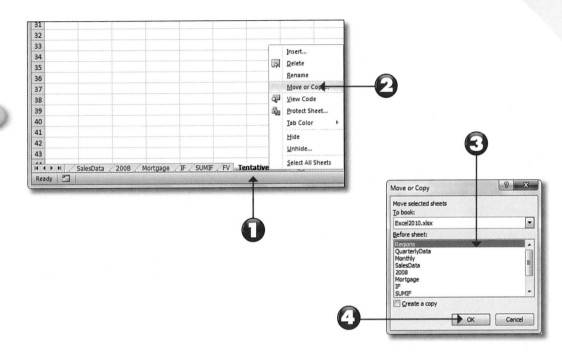

Start

1 Right-click the worksheet tab that you want to move.

2 Select **Move or Copy** from the shortcut menu. The Move or Copy dialog box opens.

3 In the list of worksheets, click the name of the worksheet in front of which you want the selected sheet to be moved.

4 Click the **OK** button to move the worksheet.

End

NOTE

Move by Dragging   You can also click on a worksheet tab and drag it in front of or after another worksheet tab to change its location. This can be a much more efficient method of moving worksheets in smaller workbooks that contain only a handful of worksheets. ■

COPYING WORKSHEETS BETWEEN WORKBOOKS

You might find that a worksheet used in one workbook would be of use in another workbook. Instead of recreating the worksheet, you can simply create a copy of the worksheet in the other workbook.

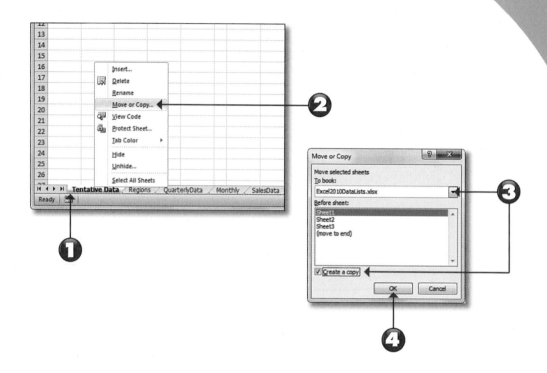

Start

End

1 Right-click the worksheet tab that you want to copy.

2 Select **Move or Copy** from the shortcut menu. The Move or Copy dialog box opens.

3 Click the **down arrow** next to the To Book field and choose the workbook to which you want the target worksheet copied. Then click the **Create a Copy** check box.

4 Click the **OK** button. At this point, Excel copies the worksheet as directed.

NOTE

Moving Versus Copying   Be sure to click the Create a Copy option when copying a worksheet. If you fail to do so, the worksheet will be moved to the other workbook instead of copied. If the worksheet is moved, it will no longer be accessible in the current workbook. ■

PASSWORD PROTECT A WORKBOOK

You may have instances where your Excel workbooks are so sensitive that only certain users are authorized to see them. In these cases, you can force your workbook to require a password to even open.

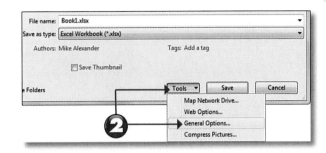

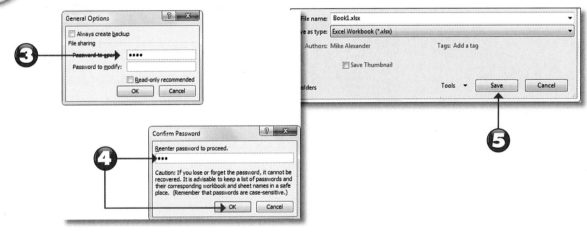

Start

1 With your workbook open, click the **File** tab and select **Save As**.

2 In the Save As dialog box, click the **Tools** dropdown and select **General Options**.

3 Enter an appropriate password in the Password to Open input box, then click the **OK** button.

4 Enter the same password in the Confirm Password dialog box, and then press the **OK** button.

5 Click the **Save** button. At this point, your worksheet is protected.

End

NOTE

Remember Your Passwords Excel offers no way to recover lost or forgotten passwords, so it's important that you remember them. If you lose or forget your password, you will have to use a third-party password-hacking program. ◾

PROTECTING A WORKSHEET

When you share files with other users, you might find it useful to protect your worksheets. When your worksheet is protected, you essentially restrict the capability to take certain actions without a password—actions such as inserting or deleting rows and cell data.

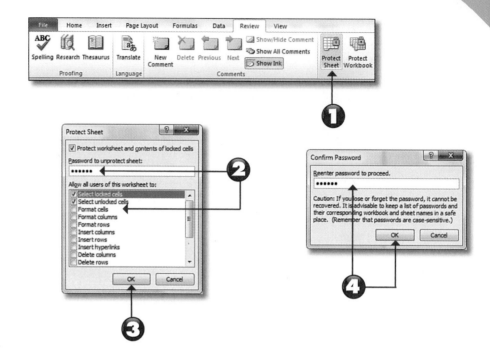

1 Go to the Review tab and select the **Protect Sheet** command.

2 Uncheck any action you want to prevent other users from performing, then enter a password in the Password text box.

3 Click the **OK** button.

4 Type the same password in the Confirm Password dialog box, then press the **OK** button. At this point, your worksheet is protected.

Continued

NOTE

The Password Is Optional   If you leave the Password entry blank, your worksheet will still be protected. However, your users will be able to unprotect the worksheet without a password. ∎

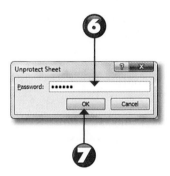

5 To unprotect a worksheet, go to the Review tab and select the **Unprotect Sheet** command.

6 Enter the password.

7 Click the **OK** button. At this point, the worksheet is unprotected.

End

NOTE

Excel Passwords are Case Sensitive   Be aware
that passwords are case-sensitive in Excel. That is, if
you enter the password as RED (uppercase letters),
your worksheet can't be unprotected if you enter
red in lowercase letters. ■

Chapter 3

ENTERING AND MANAGING DATA

Data is the technical term for the text and numbers you enter into an Excel worksheet. Each cell in an Excel worksheet can contain data made up of text, numbers, or any combination of both.

The capability to make changes to the values in your worksheet is what makes Excel such a valuable analysis tool. You can insert a cell, row, or column. You also can delete or change entries, find and replace data, and even check for spelling errors. Besides editing the data in your worksheets, you can add comments to remind yourself of information.

ENTERING DATA AND MAKING CHANGES

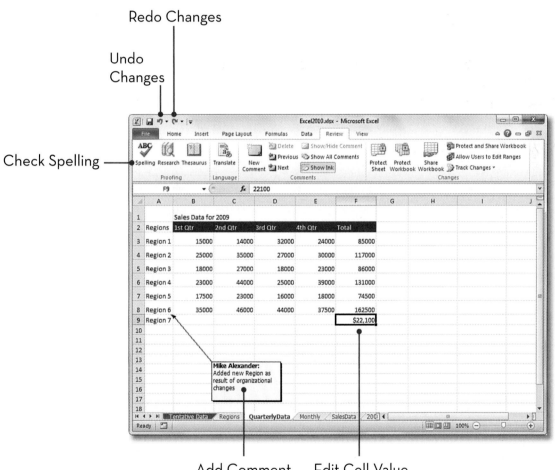

Redo Changes

Undo Changes

Check Spelling

Add Comment   Edit Cell Value

ENTERING DATA

The quickest and easiest way to get data into Excel is to enter the data via the keyboard. You can enter data into a blank worksheet or add data to an existing worksheet. For example, you can enter in the word *fruits* in cell A2 and press the Enter key.

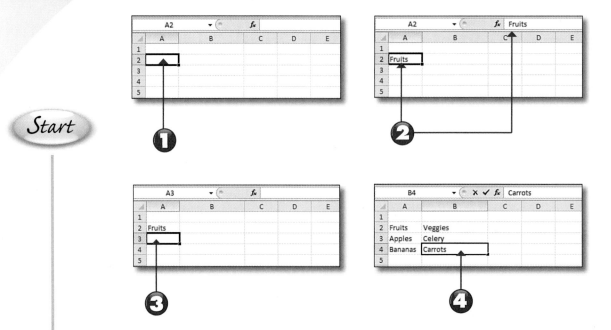

Start

① Click the cell you want to edit, making it active.

② Enter some data (in this case, **Fruits**) in the cell. As you type, the data will also show in the Edit bar.

③ Press the **Enter** key when your edit has been made. Excel makes the cell below (the one you just edited) the active cell.

④ Enter some data into a few different cells, pressing the arrow keys to move around.

End

TIP

Correcting Data While Editing   If you make a mistake while entering data, simply press the Backspace key to delete all or a portion of your entry and enter the correct data. ■

EDITING AND DELETING EXISTING DATA

You can always replace a cell's contents with new data. This comes in handy when you need to correct typing errors or when a cell contains the wrong data. You can also easily erase the contents of a cell by using the Delete key. Erasing a cell is useful when you change your mind about the contents after you enter the data in the cell.

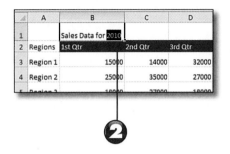

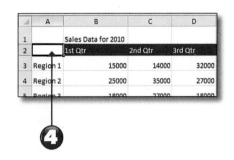

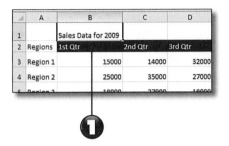

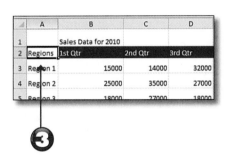

Start

1 Double-click the cell you want to edit.

2 Edit the portion of data you need changed.

3 To delete a value, click on the target cell.

4 Press the **Delete** button on your keyboard.

End

🔍 **TIP**

Use Your Arrow Keys   You can press the left and/or right arrow keys on your keyboard to move the insertion point where you want to make changes. ■

ZOOMING INTO YOUR DATA

If you want to zoom in and get a closer look at data in your worksheet, you can select a higher percentage of magnification. On the other hand, if you want to zoom out so more of the worksheet shows on the screen at one glance, select a lower percentage of magnification. Excel 2010 provides several ways to zoom in and out.

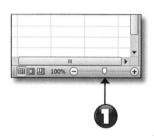

Start

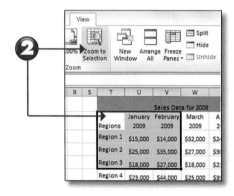

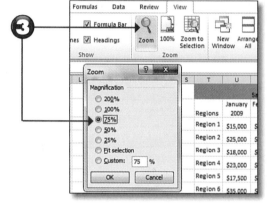

1. Slide the **Zoom Slider** on the lower-right corner of Excel. Watch your worksheet increase and reduce in magnification as you slide.

2. Select a **Range** and choose the **Zoom to Selection** command on the View tab. Note how Excel automatically increases or reduces magnification so that only that selection is visible.

3. Select the **Zoom** command on the View tab, then choose your desired magnification. After you click the **OK** button, observe how Excel applies your zoom preference.

End

TIP

Zoom with your Mouse Wheel   You can use your mouse wheel as another quick way to zoom. Hold down the Ctrl key on your keyboard while you spin your mouse wheel. This increases or reduces magnification depending on the direction you spin (up or down). ■

UNDOING AND REDOING CHANGES

If you make a mistake while working on your spreadsheet and you detect your error immediately, you can undo your action. In addition, if you undo an action by mistake, you can use Excel to quickly redo it.

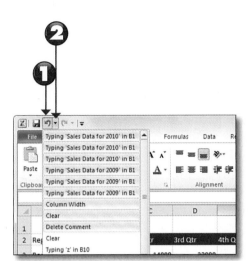

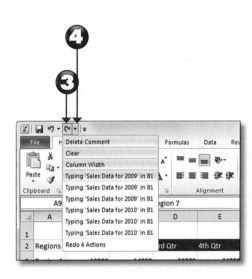

Start

1 To undo your most recent action, simply click the **Undo** icon on the Quick Access Toolbar.

2 Click on the **drop-down button** next to the Undo icon to undo all actions to a certain point.

3 To redo your most recent action, simply click the **Redo** icon on the Quick Access Toolbar.

4 Click on the **drop-down button** next to the Redo icon to redo all actions to a certain point.

End

TIP

Using Keyboard Shortcut Keys A quick and easy way to undo an action is to use the Ctrl+Z shortcut. Simply hold down the Ctrl key while pressing the Z key. You can redo an action using the Ctrl+Y shortcut. ■

COPYING AND PASTING DATA

You can avoid the trouble of retyping duplicate information in a worksheet by cutting or copying data from one part of worksheet to another. For example, if you need to duplicate a column of data, there is no need to retype that data. You can copy the data and paste it where you need it. If you want to move the column, you can cut it from its location and paste it to a new location.

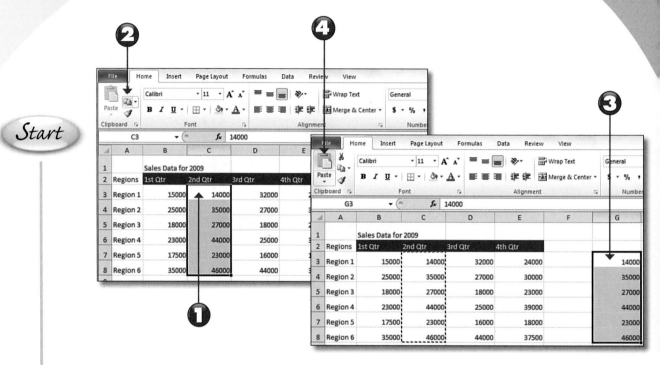

Start

① To copy and paste, click the first cell in the range you want to copy and then drag down to highlight the entire range.

② Click the **Copy** command on the Home tab.

③ Click the cell to which you want the range to be pasted.

④ Click the **Paste** command on the Home tab. Excel duplicates your range.

Continued

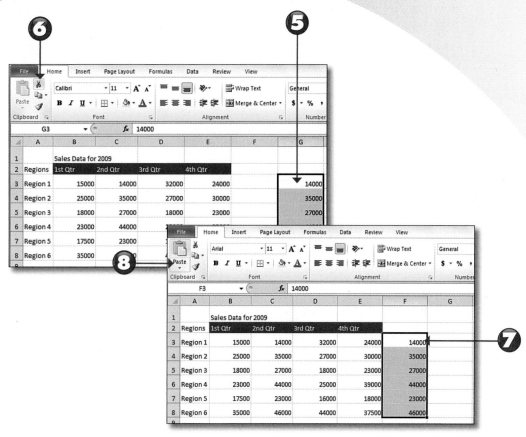

5 To copy and paste, click the first cell in the range you want to copy and then drag down to highlight the entire range.

6 Click the **Cut** command on the Home tab.

7 Click the cell you want the range pasted to.

8 Click the **Paste** command on the Home tab. Excel moves your range.

End

TIP

Using Keyboard Shortcut Keys   A quick and easy way to copy and paste data is to use the Ctrl+C and Ctrl+V shortcuts. Hold down the Ctrl key while pressing the C key to copy. Then hold down the Ctrl key while pressing the V key to paste. To cut and paste, you can use the Ctrl+X and Ctrl+V shortcut key combinations. ■

FREEZING ROWS AND COLUMNS

You might create worksheets that are so large that you cannot view all your data on the screen at the same time. In addition, if you have added row or column labels and you scroll down or to the right, you'll lose sight of your labels and which data field you're reviewing. For example, if you are reviewing sales data in columns E and F, it would be nice to see the row title of the cells you are referencing. To help, you can *freeze* the heading rows and columns so that they're always visible.

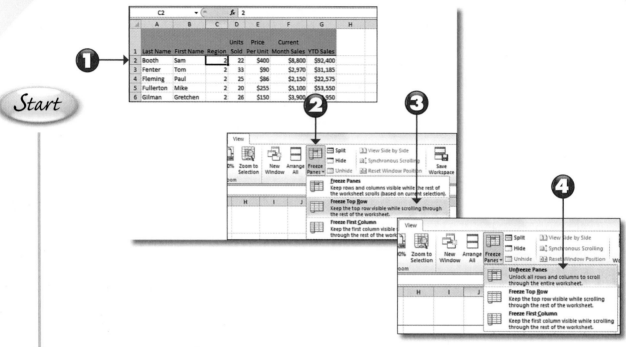

Start

1 Click in the cell below the row you want to freeze.

2 On the View tab, click the **Freeze Panes** command.

3 Click **Freeze Top Row**. At this point, you will be able to scroll down and still see the first row of your data table.

4 To unfreeze the panes, go back to the **Freeze Panes** command and click the **Unfreeze Panes** command.

End

TIP

Freezing a Column   If you are freezing a column, click the cell to the right of the column you want to freeze. Then follow the steps outlined here, but select the **Freeze First Column** command. ■

SPLITTING A WORKSHEET

By *splitting* a worksheet, you can scroll independently into different horizontal and vertical parts of a worksheet. This is useful if you want to view different parts of a worksheet or copy and paste between different areas of a large worksheet.

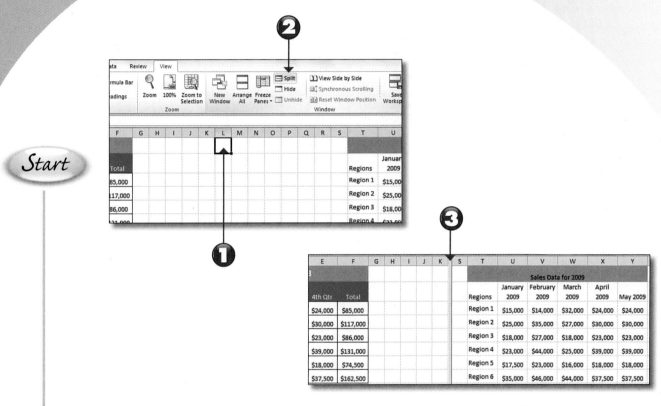

Start

① Click in the cell where you want to split the worksheet.

② On the View tab, click the **Split** command. You will now see a split bar separating your worksheet into two independently scrollable sections.

③ Move through the worksheet and see how easily you can simultaneously view other parts of the worksheet.

End

NOTE

Removing Split Bars To remove the split bars, click the Split command on the View tab. ■

INSERTING CELLS

There might be times when you need to insert new cells into the middle of your dataset. For example, if you have a table that shows data by region, you might need to insert blank cells to accommodate a new region. To avoid retyping all the data again or copying and pasting, you can insert cells and shift the current cells to their correct locations.

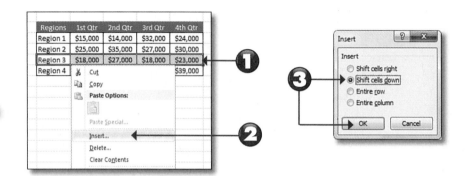

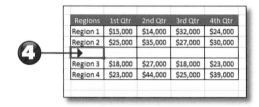

Start

1 Select the cell or cells that need to be shifted to insert new cells.

2 Right-click and choose the **Insert** option.

3 In the Insert dialog box, choose whether you want to shift existing cells right or down to make room for the new cells. Then press the **OK** button.

4 Click in your newly created cells and start adding data.

End

CAUTION

Watch for Misaligned Data When Inserting Cells Be aware that when you insert a cell, the cells below or to the right of that cell shift (one row down or one column to the right). Be careful that when this happens, your data table does not become misaligned. If it does, you may want to use the Insert Rows or Insert Columns options (explained later in this chapter). ■

DELETING CELLS

As you work with worksheets, you might find that data needs to be eliminated to keep the worksheet up to date. You can easily delete extraneous cells and shift existing cells to their correct locations.

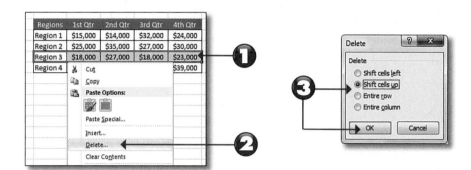

Start

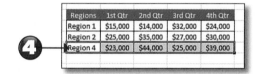

1. Select the cell or cells that need to be deleted.

2. Right-click and choose the **Delete** option.

3. In the Delete dialog box, choose whether you want to shift existing cells left or up to fill the empty space left by the deleted cells. Press the **OK** button.

4. Observe that Excel has deleted the specified cells.

End

CAUTION

Watch for Misaligned Data When Deleting Cells Be aware that when you delete a cell, the cells below or to the right of that cell shift (one row up or one column to the left). Be careful that when this happens, your data table does not become misaligned. If it does, you may want to use the Delete Rows or Delete Columns options (explained later in this chapter). ■

INSERTING AND DELETING ROWS

You can insert extra rows into a worksheet to make more room for additional data or formulas. Adding more rows, which gives the appearance of adding space between rows, can also make the worksheet easier to read. Alternatively, you can delete rows from a worksheet to close up some empty space or remove unwanted information.

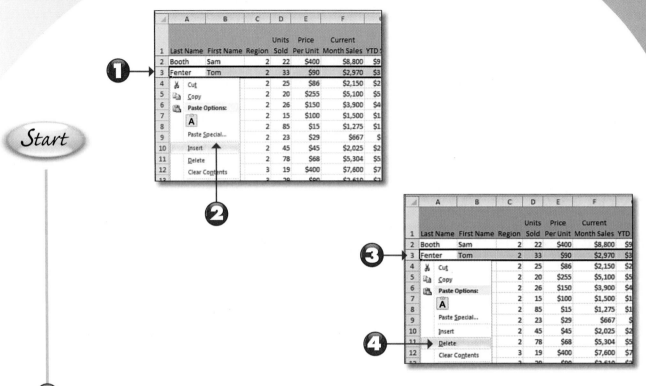

Start

1 Right-click on the row number of the existing row where you want to insert a new row.

2 Click the **Insert** option. Excel automatically adds a new row.

3 To delete a row, right-click on the row number of the existing row that you want deleted.

4 Click the **Delete** option. Excel automatically removes the specified row.

End

TIP

Hide Rows instead of Delete Rows   If there is a chance you will need the rows you are deleting, another alternative is to leave them intact—only hidden. Hide them by selecting your rows, right-clicking, and then selecting the Hide option. This way, the rows will not be visible, but you can always get them back by unhiding them. ■

INSERTING AND DELETING COLUMNS

You can insert extra columns into a worksheet to make room for more data or formulas. Adding more columns, which gives the appearance of adding space between columns, can also make the worksheet easier to read. Alternatively, you might want to delete columns from a worksheet to close up some empty space or remove unwanted information.

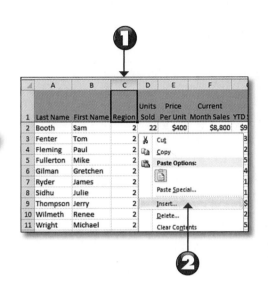

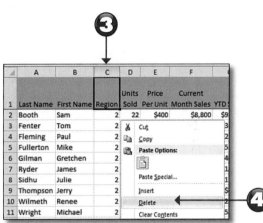

Start

1 Right-click on the column letter of the existing column where you want to insert a new column.

2 Click the **Insert** option. Excel automatically adds a new column.

3 To delete a column, right-click on the column number of the existing column that you want deleted.

4 Click the **Delete** option. Excel automatically removes the specified column.

End

TIP

Hide Columns instead of Delete Columns   You can always hide your columns instead of deleting them for good. This way, you can always get them back simply by unhiding them. Select the columns you want to hide, right-click, and then select the Hide option. To unhide, select the columns to the left and right of the hidden columns, right-click, and then select the Unhide option. ■

MOVING DATA

Excel lets you move information from one cell into another cell, which means you do not have to type the data into the new cell and then erase the data in the old location. You might want to move data in a worksheet because the layout of the worksheet has changed.

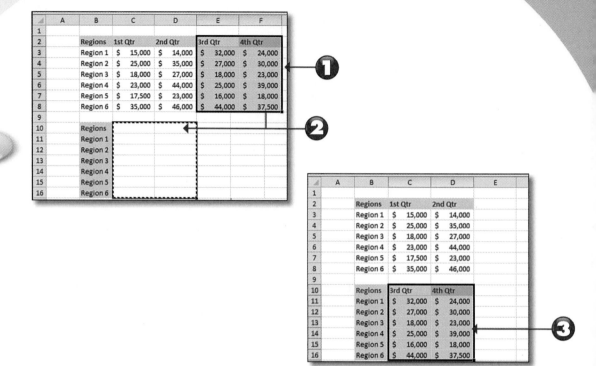

① Select the cells you want to move.

② Click the border of the selected cells and drag the cells to the location in the worksheet where you want to move the data.

③ Observe that Excel has moved your data.

Start

End

NOTE

Moving vs Cutting and Pasting   Moving data is essentially the same action as cutting and pasting data. That is, both actions allow you to move large chunks of data from one location to another. But you would typically "move" data when you need to move the data a short distance and don't want to take your hand off the mouse. ■

FINDING DATA

You will often encounter situations where you will need to find specific information in a large spreadsheet. For example, suppose you want to quickly find the row that shows the sales information for Jerry Thompson. Instead of scanning each row for the data you need, which can be time consuming, you can use Excel's Find feature.

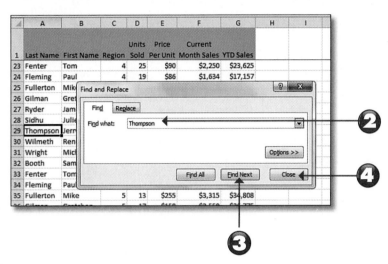

Start

 On the Home tab, click **Find and Select**, and then click **Find** or press shortcut key Ctrl+F.

2 In the Find What text box, enter the data you want to find.

3 Click the **Find Next** button. Excel finds the first instance of the data you typed and makes the cell that contains it the active cell. You can click the **Find Next** button to search for the next instance.

4 Click the **Close** button when you are done searching.

End

TIP

Finding All Instances Click the Find All button in the Find and Replace dialog box to view a list, complete with cell locations and worksheet tab names, of all the instances of the data you entered in the Find What text box. While there, you can press Ctrl+A to have Excel select all the cells in that list. ■

REPLACING DATA

Imagine that you discover some data in your table in which a company's name has been consistently misspelled, or that a salesperson you reference in a data table has changed his last name. You definitely would not want to find and replace all that data manually. Fortunately, Excel enables you to search for instances of incorrect or outdated data and replace it with new data using its Find and Replace feature.

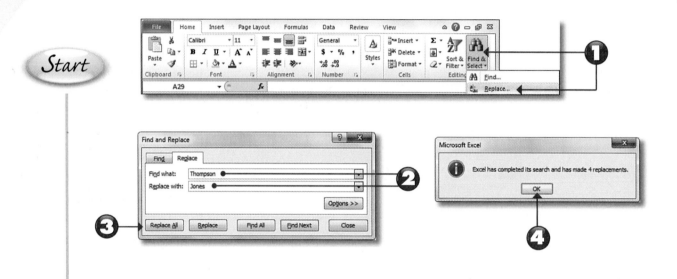

① On the Home tab, click **Find and Select** and then click **Replace**.

② In the Find What text box, type the data you would like to find. Press the Tab key to move the cursor to the Replace With text box, and type the replacement data.

③ Click **Replace All** to replace all instances of the data you typed. (Alternatively, click **Find Next** to find the first instance of the data and click **Replace** to replace it.)

④ Excel notifies you of the number of replacements it made. Click **OK**.

End

TIP

Narrowing Your Search Criteria Clicking on the Options button on the Find and Replace dialog box reveals a few options you can use to make search criteria more specific. To conduct a case-sensitive search (for example, finding all instances of "Thompson" but not "thompson"), choose the Match Case option. Choose Match Entire Cell Contents to limit your search to cells that contain no more and no less than the data you type. ■

APPLYING A DATA FILTER

When working with a large data table, it is sometimes useful to filter the table so that you can only see or work with a specific set of records. For instance, let's say you only want to see the sales reps in Region 2. When you want to work with a subset of records, you can use Excel's Filter. The Filter function allows you to see only those records that meet the criteria you select.

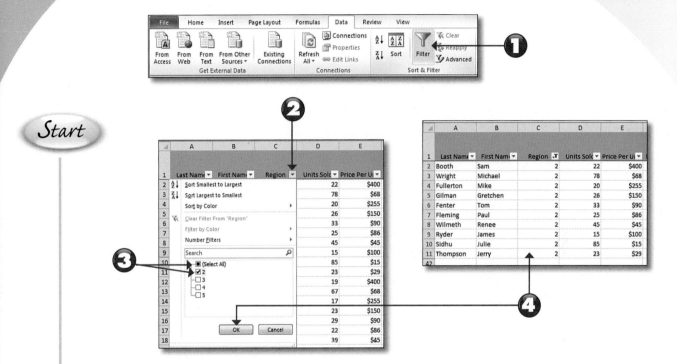

Start

End

① Click on the **Filter** command on the Data tab.

② You will immediately see filter drop-downs inside each of your header columns. Click on the drop-down selector for the column you want to filter.

③ Click the **(Select All)** option to clear all the check boxes, then click the check box next to the value by which you want to filter.

④ Click the **OK** button to apply the filter. Observe the funnel icon on the filtered column, indicating a filtered state.

TIP

Removing Data Filter Drop-downs   To remove the data filter drop-downs, simply go to the Data tab and select the Filter command. This clears all filters and eliminates the drop-downs from your header labels. ■

SORTING DATA

You will often want to change the ordering of your data. For example, you might want to sort a table of sales reps by their regions, then by YTD sales. You can meet this need by using Excel's Sort function.

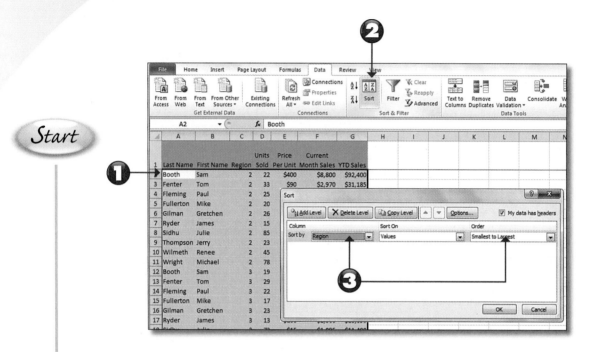

Start

① Click on any cell within the data table you are going to sort.

② On the Data tab, click the **Sort** command.

③ The Sort Dialog box opens. Select the field you want to sort and then specify whether you want to sort Smallest to Largest or Largest to Smallest.

Continued

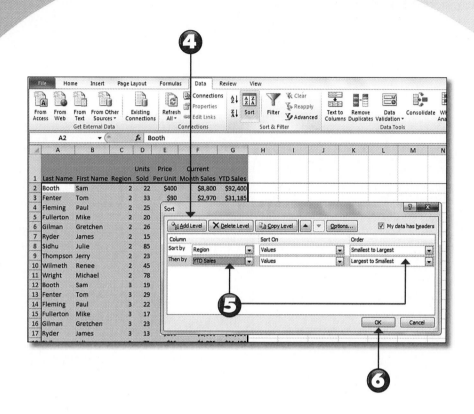

4 Click the **Add Level** button to add another level of sorting.

5 Select another field to sort by, then specify whether you want to sort Smallest to Largest or Largest to Smallest.

6 After you click the **OK** button, Excel immediately applies your custom sort.

End

ADDING AND MANAGING CELL COMMENTS

Some cells contain data that requires an explanation or special attention. Comments provide a way to attach this type of information to individual cells without cluttering the cells with extraneous information. A red triangle indicates that a cell contains a comment, which you can view in several different ways. After a comment is in place, Excel makes it easy to edit or delete it.

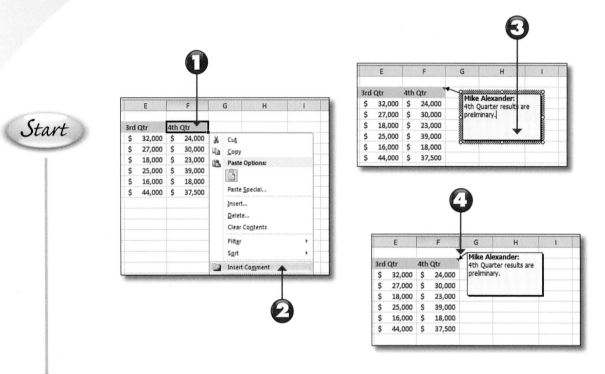

1 Right-click the cell to which you want to add a comment.

2 Select **Insert Comment**.

3 Type the desired text into the comment area. When you're finished, click anywhere in the worksheet to accept the comment.

4 The cell's upper-right corner now contains a red triangle, indicating the presence of a comment. To view the comment, hover the mouse pointer over the triangle.

Continued

TIP

Display Comments Without Hovering   You can make Excel display a cell's comments without the need to hover over the cell. To do so, right-click the commented cell and select Show/Hide Comments. To re-hide the comment, right-click the commented cell and select Hide Comment. ∎

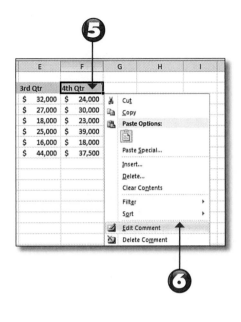

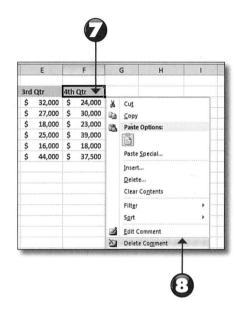

5 To edit a comment, right-click on the commented cell.

6 Select the **Edit Comment** option.

7 To delete a comment, right-click on the commented cell.

8 Select the **Delete Comment** option.

End

Chapter 4

FORMATTING WORKSHEET DATA

The primary purpose of Excel's formatting tools is to make your worksheet more readable. For example, you can change the display of the numbers so that they don't contain decimal places. This allows your audience to see the needed data without being inundated with superfluous numbers.

Excel's formatting options can be partitioned into two buckets: cell formatting and data formatting. Cell formatting is essentially the act of changing the look and feel of the cells themselves. For instance, you can change the cell background colors, add borders, change alignment, add underline or bold effects to cell contents, and wrap text. Data formatting is the act of formatting the data in the most readable and appropriate way. For example, you can format a number to show as currency complete with the dollar symbol. Or you can format a date so that it shows as Jan-10 instead of 01/01/2010.

In this chapter, you'll explore the various types of formatting you can apply to both your cells and your data.

FORMATTING NUMBERS AND TEXT

Cell Background Color

Align Text to Top of Cell

Underline

Vertical Alignment

Font Colors

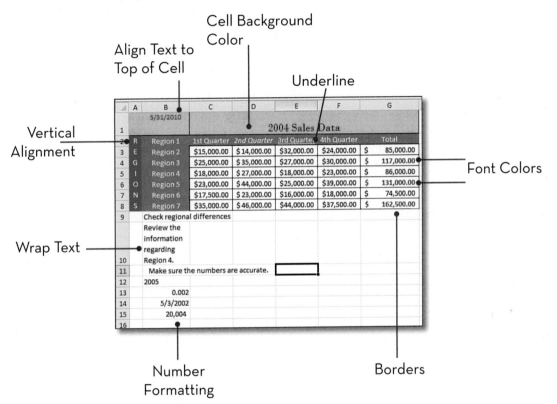

Wrap Text

Number Formatting

Borders

CHANGING THE FONT AND FONT SIZE

One way to format data in your worksheet is to change the font used to display it. This gives data a different look and feel, which can help differentiate the type of data a cell contains. You can also change the font's size for added emphasis.

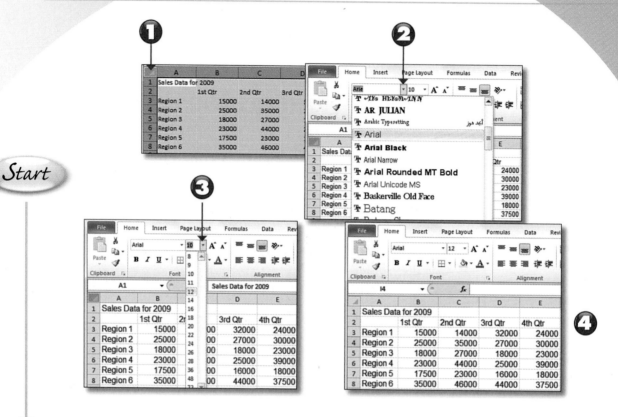

① Select the cells whose font and font size you want to change, or click the **All Cells** button (to the left of column A and above row 1) to format all the cells in the worksheet.

② Click the Font field **down arrow** in the Home tab and scroll through the available fonts. When you find the one you want to use, click it to select it.

③ Click the Font Size field **down arrow** and scroll through the available sizes (in points). When you find the size you want to use, click it to select it.

④ The font and font size you selected are applied.

TIP

Finding Font Names   If you know the name of the font you want to apply, select the down arrow next to the Font field and type the first letter of the font name. You will immediately be moved to the portion of the list that starts with the typed letter. ■

CHANGING COLUMN WIDTH

There might be times when data is too wide to be displayed within a cell, particularly if you just applied formatting to it. Excel provides several alternatives for fixing this problem. You can select columns and specify a width, or force Excel to automatically adjust the width of a cell to exactly fit its contents.

Start

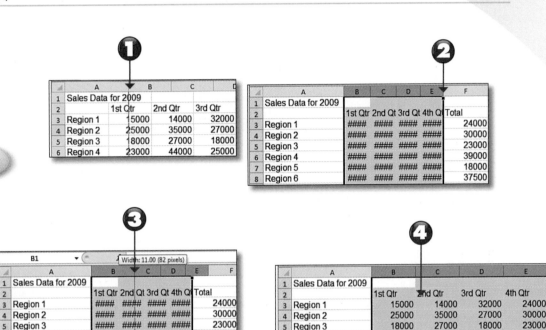

1. Move the mouse pointer over one side of the column header and then click and drag the column edge to the desired width (the column size displays in the Name Box).

2. To resize multiple columns simultaneously, select the columns that you want to alter.

3. Click and drag one of the selected columns' header edges to the desired width and release it.

4. All the selected columns are resized to the same width.

End

TIP

Quick AutoFit Column Widths Here's a quick and easy way to automatically make all columns fit their individual contents. Select the columns you want to alter, then move the cursor over the right side of the column header and double-click when the cursor changes to a two-headed arrow. Your columns will automatically snap tightly around their contents. ■

CHANGING THE COLOR OF THE CELL BACKGROUND AND CELL TEXT

Generally, cells present a white background for displaying data, but you can apply other colors or shading to the background. You can even combine these colors with various patterns for a more attractive effect. In addition, you can change the color of the data contained within your worksheet's cells.

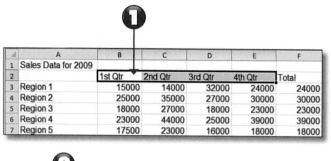

 Start

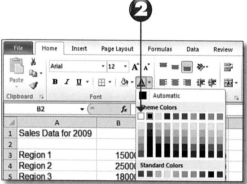

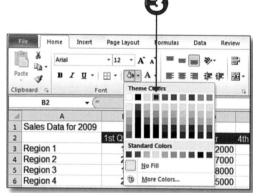

1 Select the cells whose background color and/or font color you want to change.

2 To change the color of the text in the selected cells, click the **Font Color down arrow** on the Home tab and choose a color from the list (here, white).

3 To change the color of the selected cells' background, click the **Fill Color down arrow** and choose a color from the list (here, blue). Excel applies the colors you chose.

 End

CAUTION

Choosing Colors Be sure a shading or color pattern doesn't interfere with the readability of your data. To improve readability, you might need to make the text bold or select a text color that goes well with your cells' background color. ■

TIP

Think of the Printer If you print the worksheet to a non-color printer, the color you select prints gray—and the darker the gray, the less readable the data. Yellows generally print as a pleasing light gray that doesn't compete with the data. ■

FORMATTING THE DISPLAY OF NUMERIC DATA

You can alter the display of different numbers depending on the type of data the cells contain. By formatting numeric data, you can display data in a familiar format to make it easier to read. For example, sales numbers can be displayed in a currency format, and scientific data can displayed with commas and decimals.

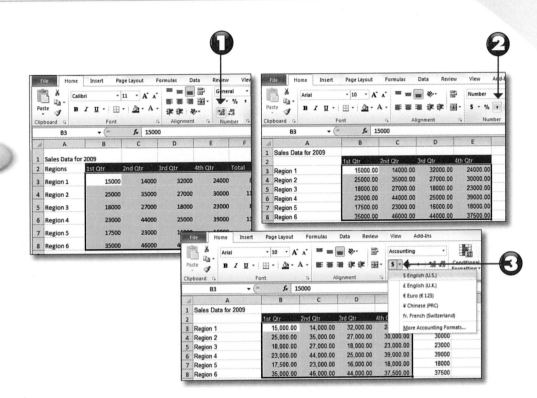

1. After you select the cells you want to format, click the **Increase Decimal** command on the Home tab twice (once for each decimal place you want displayed).

2. Click the **Comma Style** command on the Home tab to add a comma to the numeric data.

3. Click the **Currency Style** command on the Home tab to format numbers in the selected cells with a dollar sign ($), commas, a decimal point, and two decimal places.

End

TIP

Percent Style   If you click the Percent Style command on the Home tab, your numbers will be converted to a percentage, displayed with a % symbol. ■

TIP

Handling the #### Error   If, after you apply a style to cells, any cells display the error ########, it simply means that the data in the cell exceeds the current cell width. Refer to the task "Changing Column Width" in Chapter 2, "Managing Workbooks and Worksheets," to fix the problem. ■

USING A GENERAL FORMAT

When you enter numbers into Excel cells, the General format is the default. No specific number format (discussed in the next task) is applied. The General format is used when you are recording counts of items, incrementing numbers, or do not require any particular format. If you have applied another format to your cells, but want to return to this default General format, follow the steps in this task.

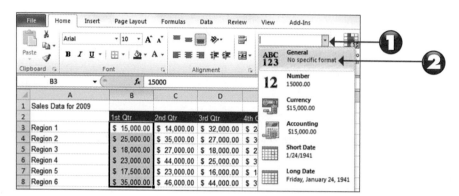

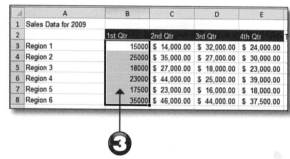

Start

1 After you select the cells you want to format, click on the **down arrow** in the **Number Format** drop-down box (on the Home tab).

2 Click the **General** option in the Category list.

3 Excel changes the format.

End

TIP

Quickly Clear All Formatting   Every now and then you may need to clear all the formatting on a sheet and start fresh. You can quickly remove all formatting by going to the Home tab and clicking Clear -> Clear Formats. ∎

USING A NUMBER FORMAT

When you apply the Number format in Excel, it uses two decimal places by default. You have the option to alter the number of decimal places, use a comma separator, and even determine the way you want negative numbers to appear (for example, with a minus sign, in red, in parentheses, or some combination of the three).

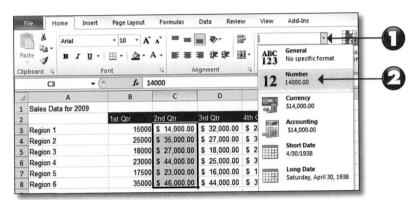

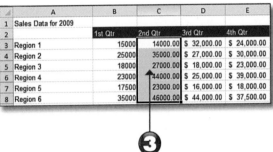

1 After you select the cells you want to format, click on the **down arrow** in the **Number Format** drop-down found on the Home tab.

2 Click the **Number** option in the Category list.

3 Excel changes the format.

End

TIP

Quickly Increase and Decrease Decimal Places   Under the Number group on the Home tab, you'll find the Increase Decimal command and Decrease Decimal command. These commands allow you to quickly change the number of decimal places used in your numbers. You can use these to easily tweak your numbers. ■

USING A CURRENCY FORMAT

When you apply the Currency format in Excel, it uses two decimal places and a dollar sign by default. You have the option to alter the number of decimal places, display a symbol for a different currency, and even determine the way you want negative numbers to appear.

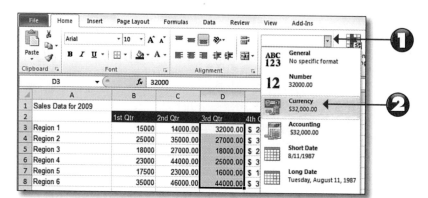

Start

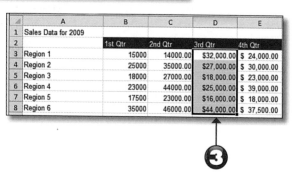

1. After you select the cells you want to format, click on the **down arrow** in the **Number Format** drop-down box on the Home tab.

2. Click the Currency option in the Category list.

3. Excel changes the format.

End

NOTE

Currency Format Options   Use the Decimal Places field in the Number tab of the Format Cells dialog box to change the number of decimal places used. To choose a different currency symbol, select it from the Symbol drop-down list. ■

NOTE

Currency-Related Formats   The Accounting format automatically lines up the currency symbols and decimal points for the cells in a column. The Percentage format multiplies the cell value by 100 and displays the result with a percent symbol. ■

USING A DATE FORMAT

When you apply the Date format in Excel, it displays the date and time serial numbers as date values. There are numerous date types you can assign to your dates. For example, you might find it easier to skim through dates as numbers with or without the assigned year visible. Or, perhaps you would rather use the actual name of the month (as opposed to a numeral) for reference.

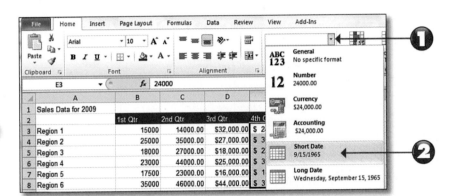

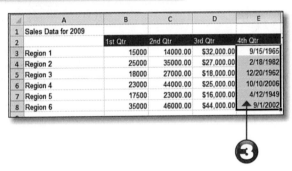

1 After you select the cells you want to format, go to the Home tab and click on the **down arrow** in the **Number Format** drop-down box.

2 Click the **Short Date** option in the Category list.

3 Excel changes the format.

End

NOTE

Using Time and Custom Formats   You can use the Time format if you want to display just the time (not the date) in your spreadsheet. In addition, you can use the Custom format option to create a Date and Time format all your own. ■

USING A TEXT FORMAT

When you type numeric data into a cell, the display defaults to a Number format. When you apply the Text format in Excel, it displays numbers as text regardless of whether the data in the cell is numeric or text-based. This can be convenient when you want to enter a number that isn't meant to be calculated or used in a mathematical operation. For instance, you may need to enter a customer number which has leading zeros. Formatting this number as text ensures that the leading zeroes remain visible.

Start

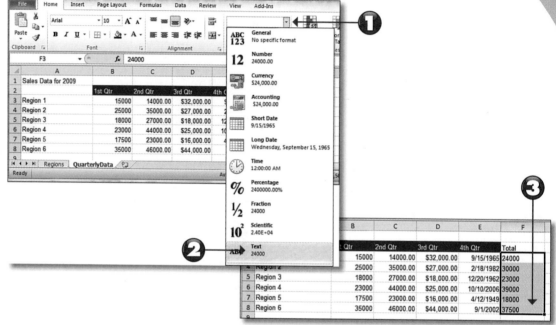

1. After you select the cells you want to format, click on the **down arrow** in the **Number Format** drop-down box (on the Home tab).

2. Click the **Text** option in the Category list.

3. Excel changes the format.

End

TIP

Immediate Number Text Another way to immediately make a number a textual cell entry is to type an apostrophe (') before you type the number. This tells Excel that the number is to be treated as text. ■

APPLYING BOLD, ITALIC, AND UNDERLINE

You can format the data contained in one or more cells as bold, italic, or underlined (or some combination of the three) to draw attention to it or make it easier to find. Indicating summary values, questionable data, or any other cells is easy with this type of formatting.

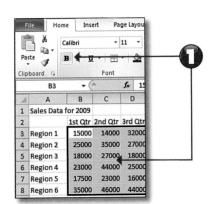

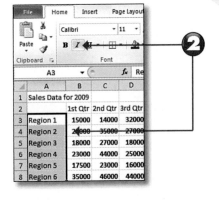

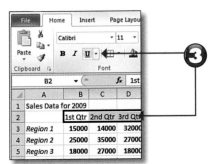

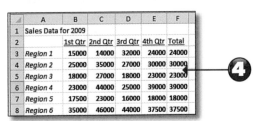

1 Select the cells in which you want to apply bold formatting and click the **Bold** command.

2 Select the cells in which you want to apply italic formatting and click the **Italic** command.

3 Select the cells in which you want to apply underline formatting and click the **Underline** command.

4 The bold, italics, and underlining are applied to the selected cells.

End

NOTE

Combination Formatting You can use several formatting techniques in combination, such as applying bold, italic, and underlining all at the same time. Simply select the text you want to format and click each of the commands on the Home tab. ■

USING MERGE AND CENTER ON CELLS

Using Excel's Merge and Center feature, you can group similar data under one heading. Columns of data usually have column headers, but they can also have group header information representing multiple columns.

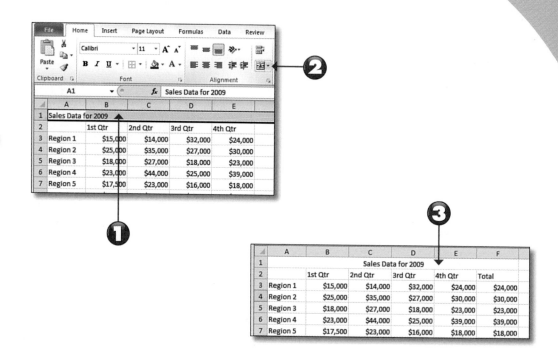

Start

1 Select the cells you want to merge together, including the cells that don't contain any data.

2 Click the **Merge and Center** command on the Home tab.

3 The cells in the group header are merged, and the data is centered. Repeat the steps in this task as needed to group additional columns in your worksheet.

End

NOTE

Unmerging Cells To unmerge or separate cells that have been merged, place your cursor in the merged cell, go to the Home tab, and click the **Merge and Center** command. ■

CHANGING HORIZONTAL DATA ALIGNMENT

Excel provides several ways to format data, and one way is to align it. The most common alignment changes you make will probably be to center data in a cell, align data with a cell's right edge (right-aligned), or align data with a cell's left edge (left-aligned). The default alignment for numbers is right-aligned; the default alignment for text is left-aligned.

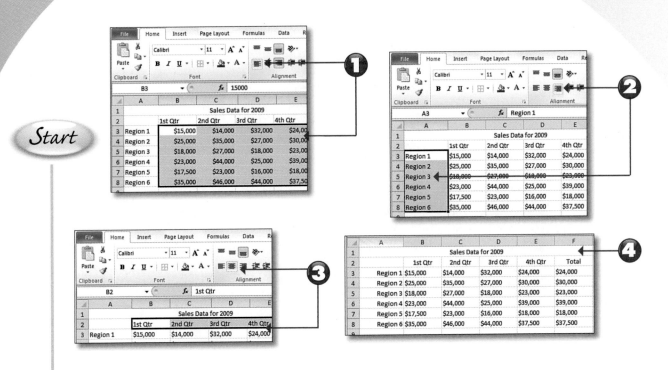

1 Select the cells in which you want to align the data to the left and click the **Align Left** command on the Home tab.

2 Select the cells in which you want to align the data to the right and click the **Align Right** command.

3 Select the cells in which you want to center the data and click the **Center** command.

4 The alignments are applied to the selected cells.

Start

End

CHANGING ROW HEIGHT

Depending on the formatting changes you make to a cell, data might not display properly. Increasing the font size or forcing data to wrap within a cell might prevent data from being entirely displayed or cause it to run over into other cells. You can frequently avoid these problems by resizing rows.

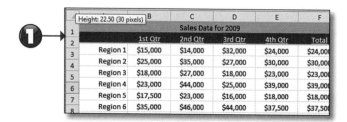

Start

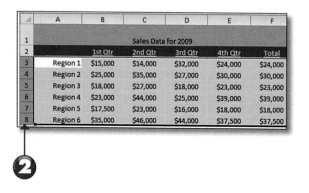

① Move the mouse pointer over the bottom edge of the row header. Click and drag the row to the desired height; the row size is displayed in the Name Box.

② To resize multiple rows simultaneously, select the rows you want to alter.

③ Click and drag one of the selected row's bottom edges to the desired height, then release it. All the selected rows are resized to the same height.

End

TIP

Quick AutoFit Rows Here's a quick and easy way to automatically make all rows fit their individual contents. Select the rows you want to alter, then move the cursor over the top border of any of the row numbers and double-click when the cursor changes to a two-headed arrow. Your rows automatically snap tightly around their contents. ■

CHANGING VERTICAL DATA ALIGNMENT

In addition to aligning the data in your cells horizontally, you can align your cell data in a vertical format. Perhaps you want the data in your cells to align to the top of the cell, the bottom of the cell, or the center of the cell, or to justify within the cell. Cell data defaults to the bottom of the cell, but you can change this according to the look you are going for.

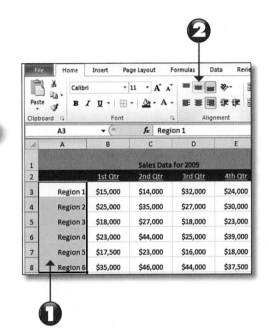

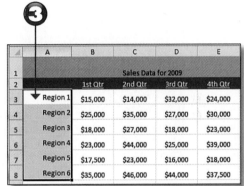

Start

1. Select the cells in which you want to align the data.

2. Go to the Home tab and click the **Middle Align** command.

3. The data is vertically aligned within the cell.

End

CHANGING CELL ORIENTATION

Excel lets you alter the orientation of cells—that is, the angle at which a cell displays information. The main reason for doing this is to help draw attention to important or special text. This feature can be convenient when you have a lot of columns in a worksheet and you don't want your column headers to take up much horizontal space, or if you simply want the information to stand out.

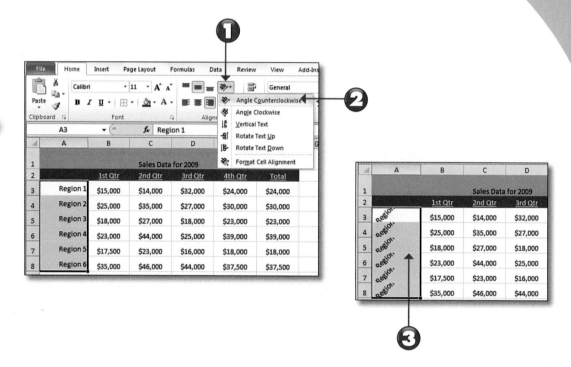

Start

1 After you select the cell or cells whose orientation you want to change, click the **Orientation** command in the Alignment group on the Home tab.

2 Choose **Angle Counterclockwise** as shown here.

3 The data reorients within the cell. (You might need to increase or decrease the height and width of the cells.)

End

TIP

Rotating Data Click the half circle in the Orientation group of the Alignment tab to quickly change the angle at which data is rotated within the selected cell(s). ■

WRAPPING DATA IN A CELL

Another way to format data is to allow text to wrap in a cell. For example, suppose a heading (row or column, for example) is longer than the width of the cell holding the data. If you are trying to make your worksheet organized and readable, it is a good idea to wrap the text in the heading so it is completely visible in a cell.

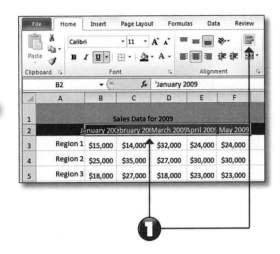

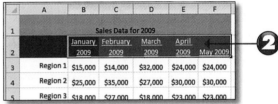

1 After you select the cell or cells whose text you want to wrap, click on the **Wrap Text** command in the Alignment group on the Home tab.

2 The data in the selected cells is automatically wrapped.

End

NOTE

Aligning Wrapped Text You might need to alter the column width to have the data wrap at the location you desire. Note that you also can align data that has been wrapped, which gives your text a cleaner look. Refer to the tasks "Changing Horizontal Data Alignment" and "Changing Vertical Data Alignment" earlier in this chapter to learn how to align data in cells. ■

CHANGING BORDERS

Each side of a cell is considered a border. These borders provide a visual cue as to where a cell begins and ends. You can customize borders to indicate other beginnings and endings, such as grouping similar data or separating headings from data. For example, a double line is often used to separate a summary value from the data being totaled. Changing the bottom of the border for the last number before the total accomplishes this effect.

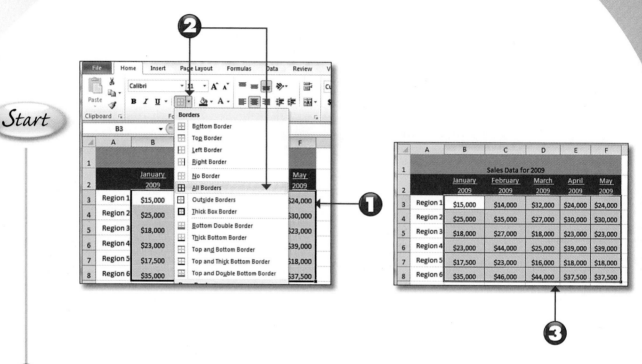

1. Select the cells to which you want to add some type of border.

2. Go to the Home tab and click the **down arrow** next to the Borders command, then choose an option from the list that appears—for example, All Borders.

3. The border is applied.

End

NOTE

Removing Borders   To remove a border, select the bordered cells, click the down arrow next to the Borders command, and choose the No Border option from the list that appears. Be careful, though; you might eliminate an intended border in a nearby cell. That's why there are all kinds of border options on the drop-down list. ■

INDENTING ENTRIES IN A CELL

Another alignment option you might want to use is to indent entries within a cell. Doing so can show the organization of entries—for example, subcategories of a budget category.

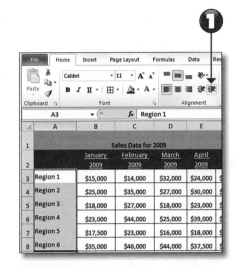

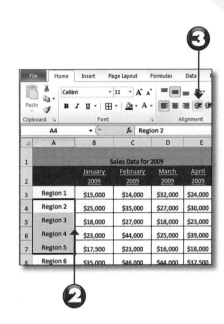

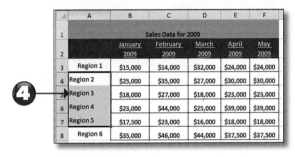

Start

① After you select the cell or range whose data you want to indent, click the Increase Indent command the number of times you want the entries indented.

② To decrease the indent, select the cell or range whose indent you want to decrease.

③ Click the Decrease Indent command to decrease the number of indents.

④ The indentation is decreased.

End

NOTE

Increasing Column Width To make the effect of the indentation stand out, you might need to increase the width of the indented column. To do so, refer to the task "Changing Column Width" earlier in this chapter. ■

CLEARING FORMATTING

Excel allows you to quickly clear all the formatting you have added to cell data, returning numbers and text to their original format.

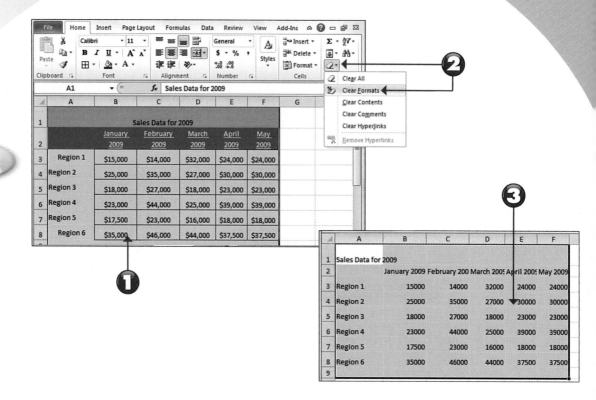

1 Select the cells whose formatting you want to clear.

2 Go to the Home tab and click on the **down arrow** next to the Clear command , and then choose Clear Formats.

3 The cell data remains, but all the formatting is gone.

End

TIP

More Clear Options If you choose Clear Contents, the formatting remains intact, but the text and data (contents) will be deleted (just as if you simply pressed the Delete key on the keyboard). If you choose Clear All, all the formatting and contents (and comments) are removed from the cell. ■

HIDING AND UNHIDING ROWS

Hiding rows is a good way to hide calculations that aren't really critical for your audience to see. You also can hide other rows that you want to include in the worksheet but don't want to display. It's kind of tricky to unhide a row because you need a way of selecting the hidden row; you'll learn how here.

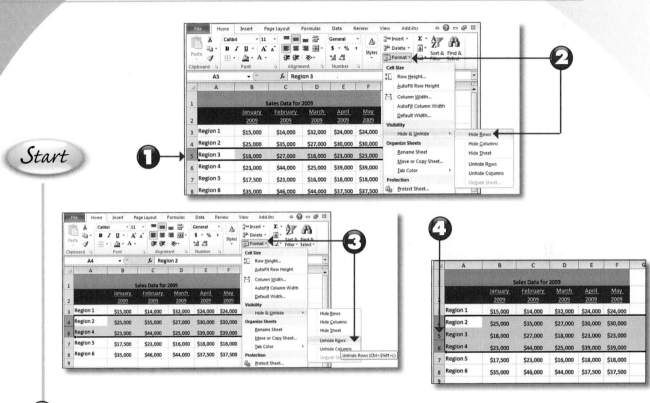

1 Click any cell in the row or the whole row that you want to hide.

2 To hide the row, click the drop-down arrow next to the Format command on the Home tab. Select **Hide & Unhide**, **Hide Rows**. (You can tell that row 5 is hidden by the jump in the row-header numbering.)

3 To unhide the row, click the drop-down arrow next to the Format command on the Home tab. Select **Hide & Unhide**, **Unhide Rows**.

4 The row is unhidden.

End

CAUTION

Printing Hidden Elements Hidden elements, whether they're rows, columns, or worksheets, don't print when you print the worksheet. ■

NOTE

Dragging to Hide Rows You also can hide a row by dragging its bottom border past the top border of the row you want to hide. ■

HIDING AND UNHIDING COLUMNS

Hiding columns is a good way to hide calculations that aren't really critical for your audience to see. You also can hide columns that you want to include in the worksheet but don't want to display. It's kind of tricky to unhide a column because you need a way of selecting the hidden column; you'll learn how here.

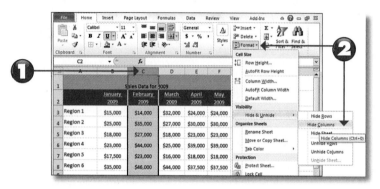

Start

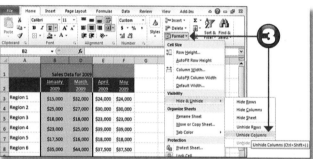

1 Click any cell in the column you want to hide.

2 To hide the column, click the drop-down arrow next to the Format command on the Home tab. Select **Hide & Unhide**, **Hide Columns**. (You can tell that column C is hidden by the jump in the column-header lettering.)

3 To unhide the column, click the drop-down arrow next to the Format command on the Home tab. Select **Hide & Unhide**, **Unhide Columns**.

4 The column is unhidden.

End

NOTE

Dragging to Hide Columns You also can hide a column by dragging its right border past the left border of the column you want to hide. ■

HIDING AND UNHIDING A WORKSHEET

Often, you'll have worksheets that are meant for your eyes only. An example of this would be a worksheet where you document changes in the workbook over the course of development. This kind of worksheet would be administrative in nature and not meant for your audience. In this scenario, hiding the worksheet would be ideal.

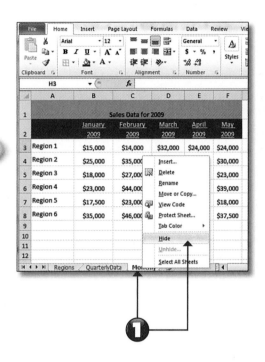

Start

End

1. After you select the tab of any sheet you want to hide, right-click on the tab and choose **Hide**. Excel hides the sheet.

2. To unhide the sheet, right-click on any tab and choose **Unhide**.

3. The Unhide dialog box opens, listing sheets that are hidden in your workbook. Double-click the worksheet name you want to unhide.

CAUTION

A Hidden Sheet is Not a Protected Sheet   Be aware that savvy users will know how to look for and unhide your hidden sheets. Do not count on hidden sheets to reliably protect sensitive information. For data protection, consider password protecting your workbook as demonstrated in Chapter 2. ■

USING FORMAT AS TABLE

Using all the formatting capabilities discussed to this point, you could format your worksheets in a very effective and professional manner—but it might take a while to get good at it. In the meantime, you can use Excel's Format As Table feature, which can format selected cells using predefined formats. This feature is a quick way to format large amounts of data and provides ideas on how to manually format data.

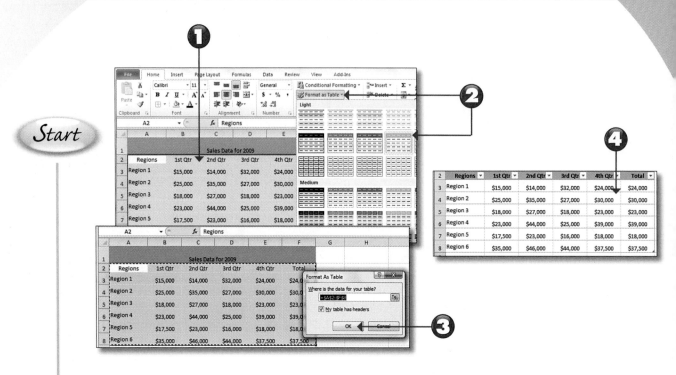

 Select the cells to which you want to apply Format As Table.

 Click on the **down arrow** next to the Format As Table command (found on the Home tab), then scroll through the available formats and click the one you want to apply to your data.

3 Click **OK** on the next pop-up to confirm that the selected range is correct.

4 The AutoFormat is applied.

End

NOTE

Modifying Format As Table   If you go to the Design tab and then run your cursor over the different styles in the Table Styles group, the selected ranges change accordingly so that you can see a preview of what that style does to the data. ■

COPYING FORMATTING

If you have taken the time to format a specific cell just so, you might decide you want to apply those same formatting options to other cells. Instead of repeating each step in the format process over and over again, you can simply use the Format Painter command.

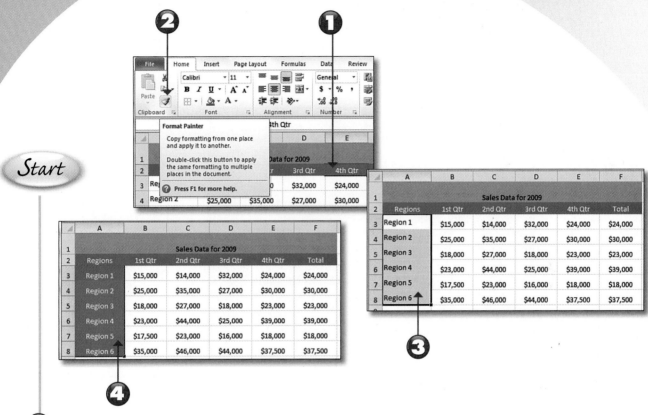

1 Click the cell with the formatting that you want to copy and apply to other cells.

2 Click the **Format Painter** command on the Home tab; the mouse pointer changes to a Format Painter pointer (paintbrush symbol).

3 Click and drag the mouse pointer to select the cells to which you want to apply the copied formatting.

4 Release the mouse command. The formatting is applied to the data in the selected cells.

TIP

Make Format Painter Persist   Double-click on the Format Painter command, (instead of single-click) and the Format Painter remains active, allowing you to format multiple areas without the need to constantly reactivate it. To turn Format Painter off, click it again. ■

CREATING AND APPLYING A FORMATTING STYLE

Instead of assigning your data an existing Excel style (for example, Normal, Currency, Percent, and so forth), you can create your own style and apply it to cells. You begin by applying the specific formatting (for example, font, font style, font size, font color, and cell color) that you want the style to have, and then give the style a specific name.

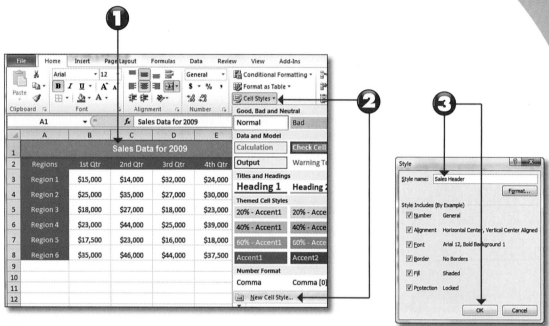

Start

① Apply any specific cell formatting that you want the style to use in your worksheet (here, Arial, Bold, 12 pt, White text, Red fill color).

② With the cell that contains the desired formatting selected, click on the **down arrow** next to the Cell Styles command on the Home tab then go to the bottom and choose **New Cell Style**.

③ Type a descriptive name for the new style in the Style name field (for example, **Sales Header**) and click **OK**.

Continued

NOTE

Saving the Style   The next time you exit Excel, you will be notified that you made a change to your global template and asked if you want to save the changes. If you want to keep the style you just created, click the Yes button; otherwise, click the No button. ■

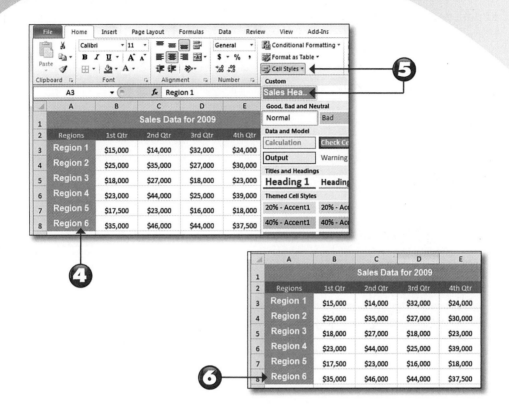

4 Select the cell(s) to which you want to apply your newly created style.

5 With the cells that you want to apply the custom style to selected, click on the **down arrow** next to the Cell Styles command on the Home tab and then choose the Sales Header style in the Custom style group at the top.

6 The style is applied to the cells you selected.

End

NOTE

Default Styles Notice that there are also default styles for Data and Model, Titles and Headings, Themed Cell Styles, and Number Format. You can run your cursor over each option to see how it changes your data prior to selecting it. ■

USING CONDITIONAL FORMATTING

There might be times when you want the formatting of a cell to depend on the value it contains. For this, use conditional formatting, which lets you specify conditions that, when met, cause the cell to be formatted in the manner defined for that condition. If none of the conditions are met, the cell keeps its original formatting. For example, you can set a conditional format such that if sales for a particular month are above $30,000, the data in the cell is bold and red.

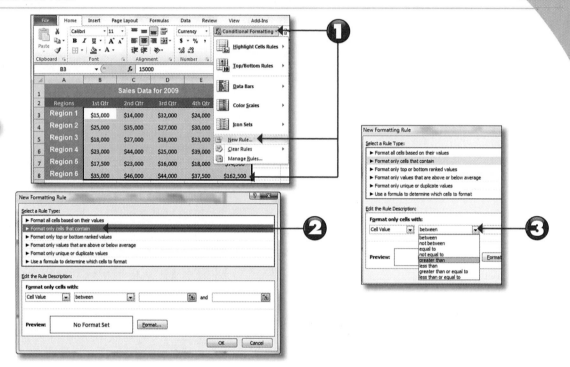

Start

1 Select the cells to which you want to apply conditional formatting, then click on the **down arrow** next to the Conditional Formatting command on the Home tab and choose **New Rule**.

2 In the conditional Formatting dialog box, choose the **Format only cells that contain** option.

3 Leave the first drop-down list as Cell Value. Display the second drop-down list to select the type of condition (for example, greater than).

Continued

NOTE

Painting a Format Onto Other Cells   You can copy the conditional formatting from one cell to another. To do so, click the cell whose formatting you want to copy and hen click the Format Painter command. Finally, drag over the cells to which you want to copy the formatting. ∎

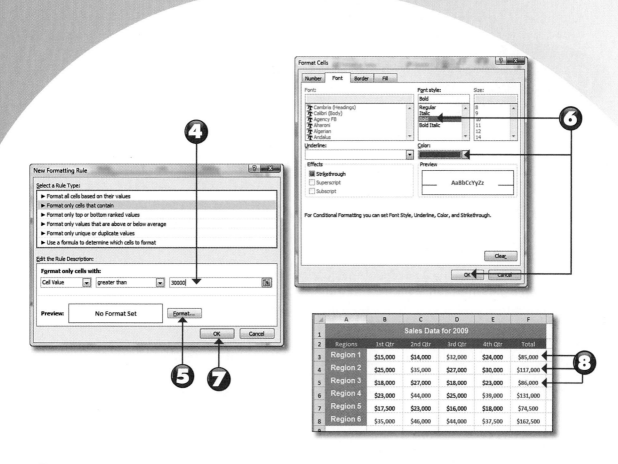

4 Type the value of the condition (the number that the cells must be "greater than").

5 Click the **Format** command to set the format to use when the condition is met.

6 Click the options you want to set in the Format Cells dialog box (for example, **Pink** in the Color field and **Bold** in the Font style list), and click **OK**.

7 Click **OK** in the Conditional Formatting dialog box.

8 Excel applies the formatting to any cells that meet the condition you specified.

End

NOTE

When to Use Conditional Formatting   Use conditional formatting to draw attention to values that have different meanings, depending on whether they are positive or negative, such as profit and loss values. ■

Chapter 5

WORKING WITH FORMULAS AND FUNCTIONS

A *formula* is essentially a series of instructions you give Excel to return a value. These instructions can be mathematical operations, or a call to a built-in Excel function. Excel typically displays the result of a formula in a cell as either numeric or textual data.

Functions are abbreviated formulas that perform specific operations on a group of values. Excel provides more than 250 functions that can help you with tasks ranging from determining loan payments to calculating investment returns. For example, the SUM function automatically adds up the numeric values within a given range.

In this chapter, you will walk through the ins and outs of using Excel formulas and functions. By the end of this chapter, you will be well equipped to start building your own formulas!

FUNCTIONS AND CORRECTING ERRORS

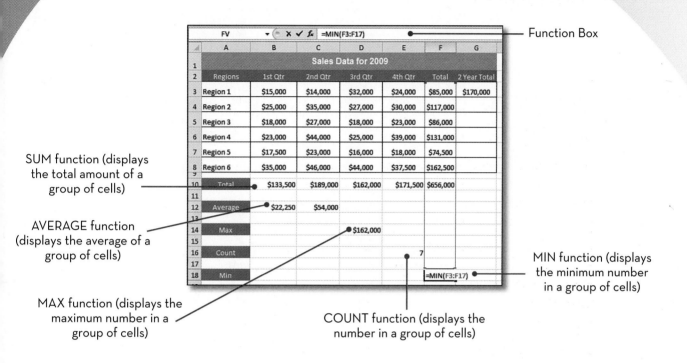

Function Box

SUM function (displays the total amount of a group of cells)

AVERAGE function (displays the average of a group of cells)

MAX function (displays the maximum number in a group of cells)

COUNT function (displays the number in a group of cells)

MIN function (displays the minimum number in a group of cells)

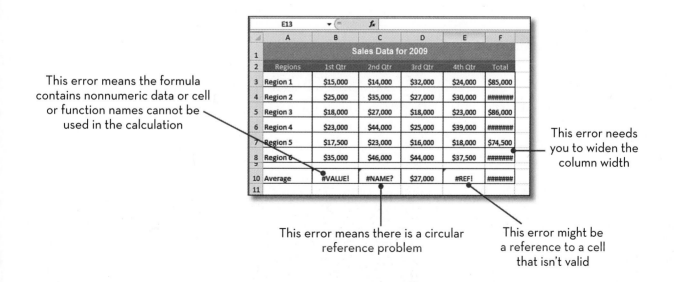

This error means the formula contains nonnumeric data or cell or function names cannot be used in the calculation

This error needs you to widen the column width

This error means there is a circular reference problem

This error might be a reference to a cell that isn't valid

USING AUTOSUM (SUM)

Excel can use formulas to perform calculations for you. Because a formula refers to cells rather than to the values those cells contain, Excel updates the sum whenever you change the values in the cells. You'll probably use the AutoSum formula a lot—it adds numbers in a range of cells.

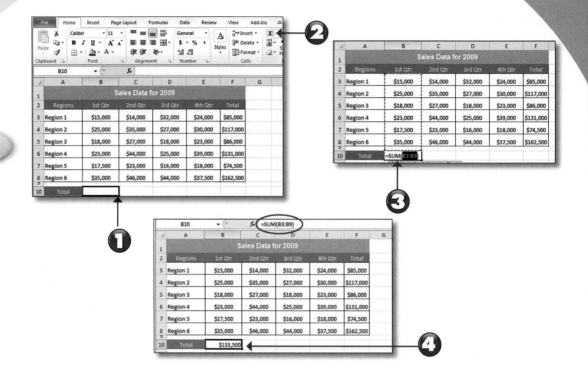

Start

End

1. Click in the cell in which you want the result of the AutoSum operation to appear (this is called the *resultant cell*).

2. Click the **AutoSum** command on the Home tab.

3. Excel selects the most obvious range of numbers and puts a dotted line around the cells. Press **Enter** to accept the range or use the mouse to select alternative cells.

4. Click the resultant cell to make it the active cell. Notice that the formula is displayed in the Formula bar.

TIP

AutoSum Shortcut Key   Excel provides an easy way to implement the AutoSum via a shortcut key. Using your keyboard, enter the combination of Alt and the Plus symbol (+). You'll see that Excel performs the AutoSum for you. At that point, just press the Enter key on your keyboard to accept the AutoSum calculation. ■

FINDING A CELL AVERAGE (AVERAGE)

A function is one of Excel's many built-in formulas for performing a specialized calculation on the data in your worksheet. For example, instead of totaling your sales data, you can use Excel's AVERAGE function to determine the average of each quarter per region.

Start

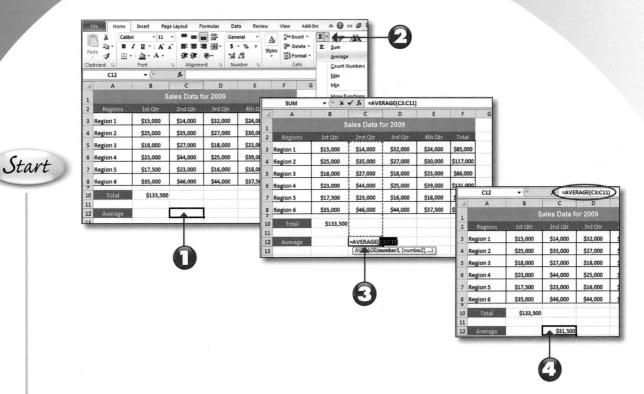

① Click the cell in which you want the result of the AVERAGE function to appear (this is called the *resultant cell*).

② Click the **down arrow** next to the AutoSum command on the Home tab and choose **Average** from the list that appears.

③ Excel selects the most obvious range of numbers and puts a dotted line around the cells. Press **Enter** to accept the range or use the mouse to select alternative cells.

④ Click the resultant cell to make it the active cell. Notice that the formula is displayed in the Formula bar.

End

NOTE

Selecting Specific Cells for your Calculation   If you don't want to use the range of cells that Excel selects for you, click on the first cell you want, hold down the Ctrl key, and click on each additional cell you would like to include in the calculation. When you finish selecting the cells you want to calculate, press Enter to see the result. ■

FINDING THE LARGEST CELL AMOUNT (MAX)

As its name suggests, the MAX function returns the largest/maximum number in any given range. You would typically use this function if you needed to dynamically reference the largest number in other formulas. You can use Excel's MAX function to, for example, determine the quarter in which you had the most sales. Although it's easy enough to see this information with your eyes, the Quarter with the most sales changes as each quarter passes. Instead of manually keeping up with which quarter is the king of sales, the MAX function does that for you.

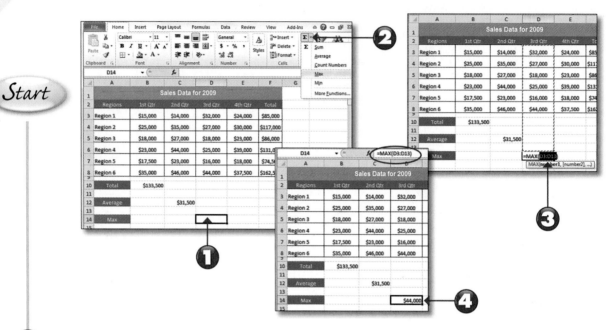

Start

1 Click the cell in which you want the result of the MAX function to appear (this is called the *resultant cell*).

2 Click the **down arrow** next to the AutoSum command on the Home tab and choose **Max** from the list that appears.

3 Excel selects the most obvious range of numbers and puts a dotted line around the cells. Press **Enter** to accept the range or use the mouse to select alternative cells.

4 Click the resultant cell to make it the active cell. Notice that the formula is displayed in the Formula bar.

End

NOTE

Finding the Minimum Cell Amount In addition to enabling you to find the largest cell amount, you can also find the smallest cell amount. See the next task, "Finding the Smallest Cell Amount (MIN)," for more information. ■

FINDING THE SMALLEST CELL AMOUNT (MIN)

As its name suggests, the MIN function returns the largest/maximum number in any given range. This is the direct opposite of the MAX function, which returns the largest number in a range. You would typically use Excel's MIN function to determine the lowest performing Region, or Market, or whatever else you're measuring. This quickly gives you a reference point for the lowest number you're dealing with in your data.

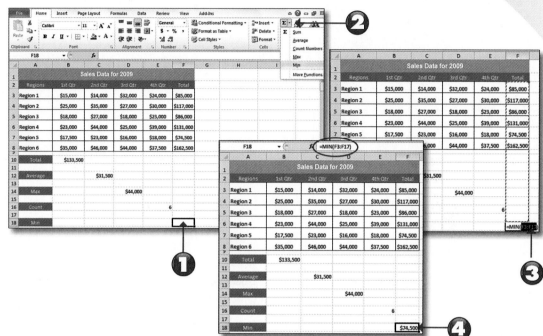

Start

End

1 Click the cell in which you want the result of the function to appear (this is called the *resultant cell*).

2 Click the **down arrow** next to the AutoSum command on the Home tab and choose **Min** from the list that appears.

3 Excel selects the most obvious range of numbers and puts a dotted line around the cells. Press **Enter** to accept the range or use the mouse to select alternative cells.

4 Click the resultant cell to make it the active cell. Notice that the formula is displayed in the Formula bar.

NOTE

Finding the Maximum Cell Amount In addition to enabling you to find the smallest cell amount, you can also find the largest cell amount. Refer to the task "Finding the Largest Cell Amount (MAX)" earlier in this chapter for more information. ∎

COUNTING THE NUMBER OF CELLS (COUNT)

As you may have guessed, the COUNT function literally counts the number of data points in any given range. Suppose you want to know how many values (data points) are in your data table—you could use Excel's COUNT function to count the number of cells in a selected range.

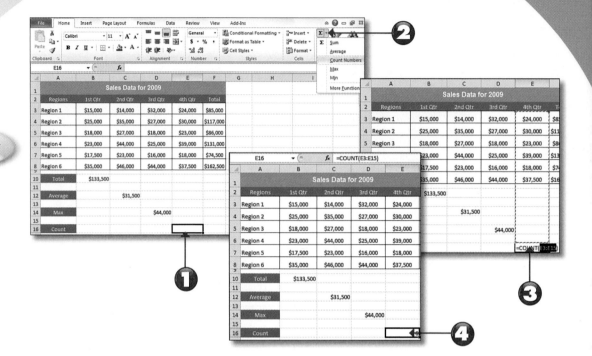

Start

1 Click the cell in which you want the result of the COUNT function to appear (this is called the *resultant cell*).

2 Click the **down arrow** next to the AutoSum command on the Home tab and choose **Count Numbers** from the list that appears.

3 Excel selects the most obvious range of numbers and puts a dotted line around the cells. Press **Enter** to accept the range or use the mouse to select alternative cells.

4 Click the resultant cell to make it the active cell. Notice that the formula is displayed in the Formula bar.

End

TIP

Counting Text Values You'll notice that the COUNT function only works if the range you are counting is numbers based. To count the data points in a range that contains either numbers or text, you can use the COUNTA function. To use COUNTA, edit your COUNT formula to add an A. ■

ENTERING A FORMULA

Another way to use a formula is to type it directly into the cell. You can include any cells in your formula; they do not have to be next to each other. Also, you can combine mathematic operations—for example, C3+C4–D5.

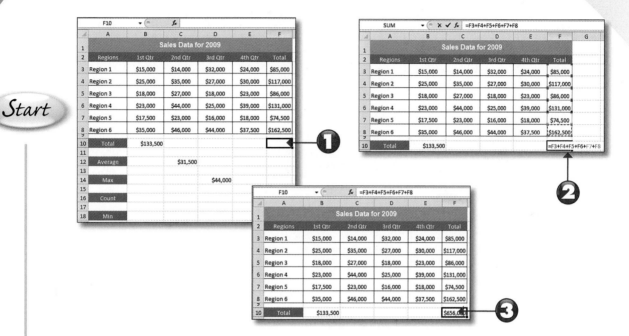

1 Click the cell in which you want the result of the formula to appear (this is called the *resultant cell*).

2 Type **=** (the equal sign) followed by the references of the cells containing the data you want to total (for example, F3+F4+F5+F6+F7+F8), and then press **Enter**.

3 Click the resultant cell to make it the active cell; the values in the specified cells are added together.

End

CAUTION

Order of Operation   Excel first performs calculations within parentheses, and then it performs multiplication or division calculations from left to right. Finally, it performs any addition or subtraction from left to right. ◼

EDITING A FORMULA OR FUNCTION

After you enter a formula or function, you can change the values in the referenced cells, and Excel automatically recalculates the value based on the changes. You can include any cells in a formula or function; they do not have to be next to each other.

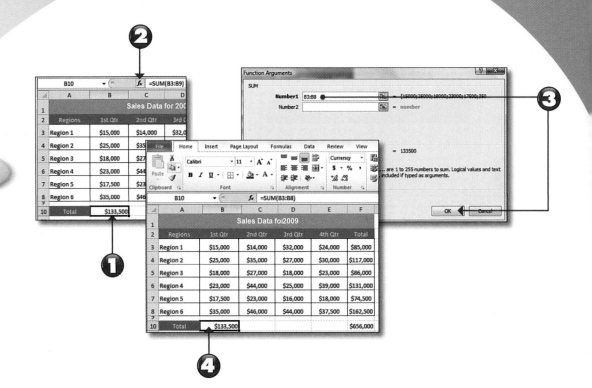

Start

1 Click the cell you want to edit; the function is displayed in the Formula bar.

2 Click the **Insert Function** command on the Formula bar to open the Function Arguments dialog box. (If a formula, the Insert Function dialog box will appear.)

3 Type the changes to your function. For example, change the cells being summed to B3-B8 instead of B3-B9. Then click **OK**.

4 The changes are made and the result appears in the cell.

End

TIP

Pressing F2 Instead of using the Function Arguments dialog box to edit your formulas, you can press the F2 key and edit your formula just like you would for regular text or data on the Formula bar. ■

COPYING A FORMULA

When you build your worksheet, you might want to use the same data and formulas in more than one cell. With Excel's Copy command, you can create the initial data or formula once and then place copies in the appropriate cells. For example, suppose you want to find the average sales per quarter in other sales regions. To do so, create the formula for the first region, and copy it to cells for the other regions. Excel automatically figures out how to change the cell ranges to which the formula should apply.

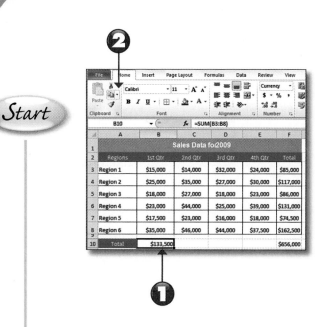

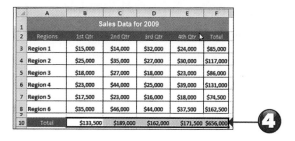

1 Click the cell that contains the function you want to copy.

2 Click the **Copy** command on the Home tab; a line surrounds the cell you are copying.

3 Click the cell or cells into which you want to paste the formula.

4 Press **Enter** (or Ctrl+V) to paste the formula into each of the selected cells.

End

TIP

Increasing Cell Width If you paste a copied formula, you might need to alter the size of your columns to accommodate the new size of the data in the cell. To automatically make an entire column (or multiple columns) fit the width of the widest cell in that column (or columns), move the cursor over the right side of the column header and double-click when the cursor changes to a two-headed arrow. ■

ASSIGNING NAMES TO A CELL OR RANGE

You can create range names that make it easier to create formulas and move to that range. For example, a formula that refers to a range named Qtr1 is easier to understand than one named B4:B9. Not only is it easier to remember a name than the cell addresses, but Excel also displays the range name in the Name box—next to the Formula bar. You can name a single cell or a selected range in the worksheet.

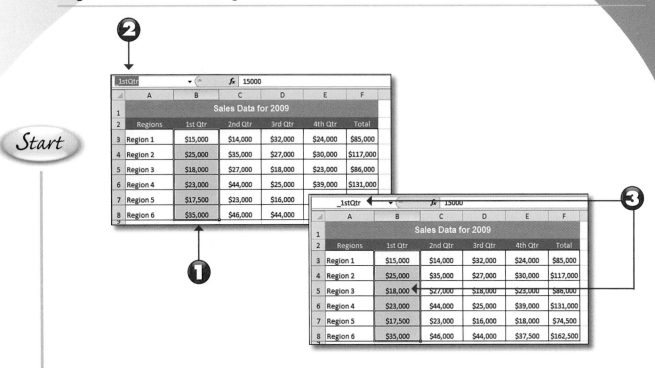

Select the cell or range you want to name.

Click in the **Name** Box, type the desired range name, and press **Enter**.

Excel names the range. When the range is selected, the name appears in the Name box.

Start

End

TIP

Rules for Naming Ranges Excel has a few basic rules for the naming of ranges. You must start your range names with a letter or an underscore. You can use numbers anywhere else in your range names, but no spaces. You can also use up to 255 characters, but as a best practice, you should always strive to keep your range names short and pithy. Finally, you cannot use a name that conflicts with a built-in range or cell reference. For example, you can't use A1 as a range name. ■

REFERENCING NAMES IN A FUNCTION

One of the reasons you create a name for a cell or group of cells is so that you can easily refer to that cell or range in a function. That way, rather than typing or selecting a range or cell, you can type the name or select it from the Paste Name dialog box.

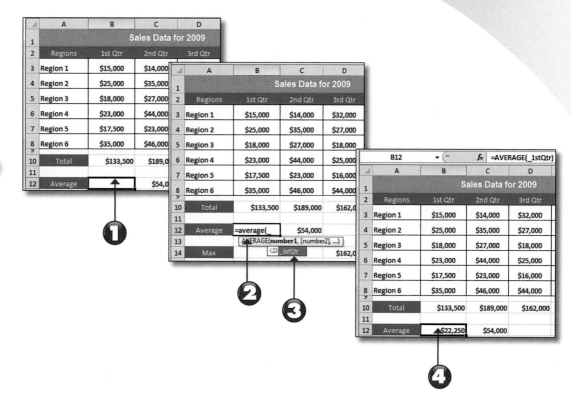

Start

1 Click in the cell in which you want the result of the formula to appear (this is called the *resultant cell*).

2 Type the function in the cell using a named cell or range—for example, **=AVERAGE(_1stQtr)**. As you type the name, you should see a list of named ranges pop up below the cell.

3 You can click on one to select it.

4 Press the **Enter** key.

End

NOTE

Quickly Retrieve a Range Name If you forget the name of a range while you are typing a formula, go to the Formula tab and click the Use in Formula dropdown. This gives you a list of the available ranges. Click the one you are looking for and the range name is automatically placed in the formula. ■

NOTE

Deleting a Range Name To delete a range name, go to the Formulas tab and click on the Name Manager. There, you can click on the target range name and click the Delete command. Click OK to confirm the deletion. ■

USING FUNCTIONS ACROSS WORKSHEETS

You can use cell references from other worksheets in your calculations. For example, suppose you have two worksheets that contain the calculations for the total sales by region for a particular year. In a third worksheet, you want to calculate the total sales by region for the last two years. You can reference the cells in the first two worksheets that contain the totals and perform calculations on them in the third worksheet.

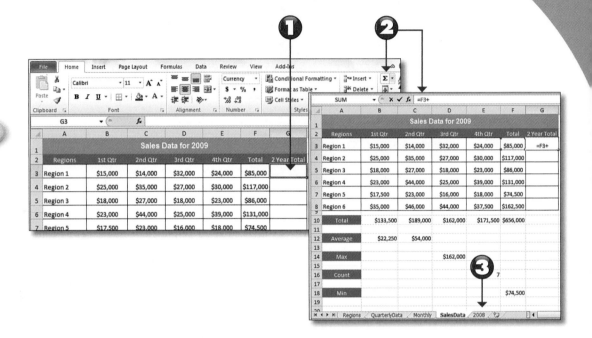

Start

1. Click in the cell in which you want the result of the formula to appear (this is called the *resultant cell*).

2. In this example, we are going to add the sum of this operation to last year's data in another worksheet (2008), so we start our formula referencing the 2009 total, then we enter a **+** (plus sign).

3. Click the tab of the worksheet that contains the cell you want to reference in the calculation.

Continued

TIP

Using Worksheet Name References   Instead of switching back and forth between worksheets, you can manually type the reference to the worksheet name directly in your formulas. Select the location of the cell in a particular worksheet (column letter and row number) in addition to the sheet name—for example, Sheet1!A1. If your sheet name contains spaces, you will need to wrap your sheet name with a single quote – for example, 'My Second Sheet'!A1. ■

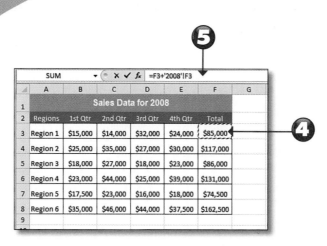

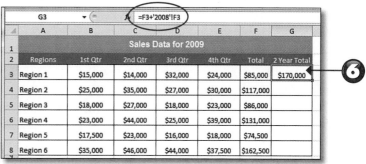

④ Click the cell that you want to use in your calculation; it appears next to the worksheet name in the Formula bar.

⑤ Press the **Enter** key. Excel performs the calculation and returns you to the original worksheet.

⑥ Click the resultant cell to make it the active cell. Notice that the function is in the Formula bar.

End

CAUTION

Be Aware of Worksheet Name References   Each cell you reference from another worksheet must be prefaced with its worksheet name. For example, if you have the formula =SUM(Sheet1!A1+B1) in cell C3 of Sheet2, this references cell A1 from Sheet1 and B1 from Sheet2. If you need to reference both A1 and B1 from Sheet 1, you must include the worksheet name with both cell references, like so: =SUM(Sheet1!A1+Sheet1!B1). ▪

USING AUTO-CALCULATE

Suppose you want to see a function performed on some of your data—in this example, to determine the lowest quarterly sales goal of any region in 2009—but you don't want to add the function directly into the worksheet. Excel's Auto-Calculate feature can help.

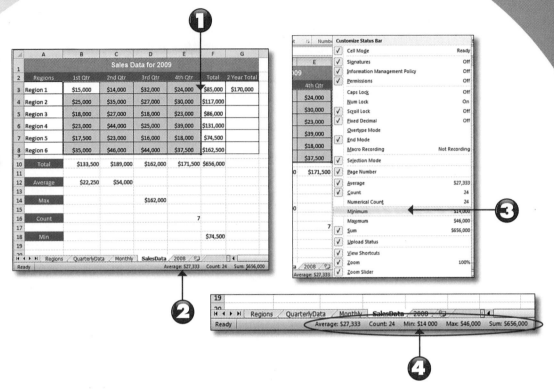

Start

End

① Select the cells that you want to Auto-Calculate.

② The Status Bar now shows you the Average, Count, and Sum.

③ Right-click the **Status Bar** and click on each option you want to enable or disable.

④ Observe your new Auto Calculation(s).

NOTE

Turning Off Auto-Calculate   You can turn off the Auto-Calculate feature by right-clicking on the Status Bar and unselecting each option that is selected. ■

FINDING FUNCTIONS

In the old days, you had to know the name of the function you wanted to use. Now, however, Excel makes it easy to find the function you need—all you have to know is what you want the function to do.

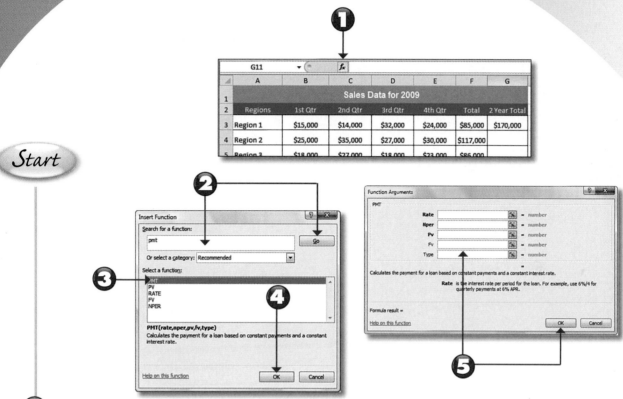

 Start

1 Click the **Insert Function (fx)** command next to the Formula bar.

2 Type a description of the function you are looking for in the Search For a Function text box and press **Enter** (or click the **Go** command).

3 Scroll through the list in the Select a Function box and select a function to read a description of it.

4 When you find the function you are looking for, click **OK**.

5 Excel walks you through the process of entering the function's arguments in the Function Arguments dialog box. Click **OK** when you are done entering its arguments.

End

NOTE

Function Arguments Help   If you need help while you are entering your function arguments, click the Help On This Function link in the bottom-left corner of the Function Arguments dialog box. ■

CALCULATING A LOAN PAYMENT (PMT)

Using Excel, you can determine a monthly loan payment based on a constant interest rate, a specific number of pay periods, and the current loan amount.

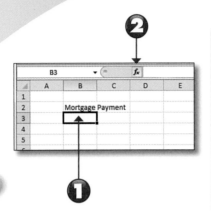

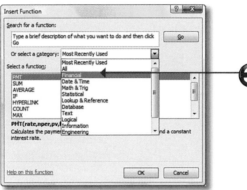

1 Click in the cell in which you want the result of the function to appear (this is called the *resultant cell*).

2 Click the **Insert Function (fx)** command next to the Formula bar.

3 The Insert Function dialog box opens. Click the **down arrow** next to the Or Select a Category field and choose **Financial** from the list that appears.

4 A list of financial-related functions appears in the Select a Function list. Scroll through the list to locate the PMT function and double-click it.

Continued

NOTE

Function Arguments Help If you need help while entering function arguments, click the Help On This Function link in the bottom-left corner of the Function Arguments dialog box. ■

NOTE

Negative Payment Your resulting payment is a negative number because payments are considered a debit. ■

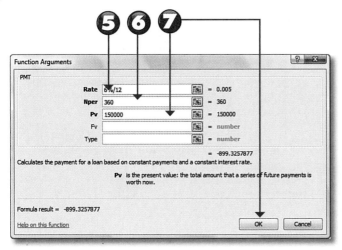

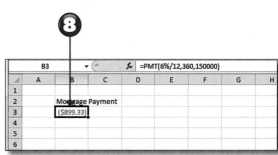

5 In the Rate field, type the interest rate per period. For example, type **6%/12** for monthly payments on a 6% annual percentage rate (APR).

6 In the Nper field, type the total number of loan payments. For example, type **360** if you'll be making 12 payments per year on a 30-year loan.

7 In the Pv field, type the present value of the loan—for example, **150,000**—and click **OK**.

8 Excel calculates the payment and inserts it in the resultant cell.

End

NOTE

Type Argument   If you don't enter a number in the Type argument, it defaults to 0, which means that the last payment will pay off the mortgage loan (this is because mortgages are paid in arrears—at the end of the payment period). If you are calculating a car payment, you might put a 1 in the Type argument because you make your payments at the beginning of the payment period. A 1 versus a 0 makes a slight difference in the calculation because of the interest accrued. ■

PERFORMING A LOGICAL TEST FUNCTION (IF)

Using Excel, you can perform a logical test function—for example, to indicate whether scores equal a passing or failing grade based on an established set of criteria.

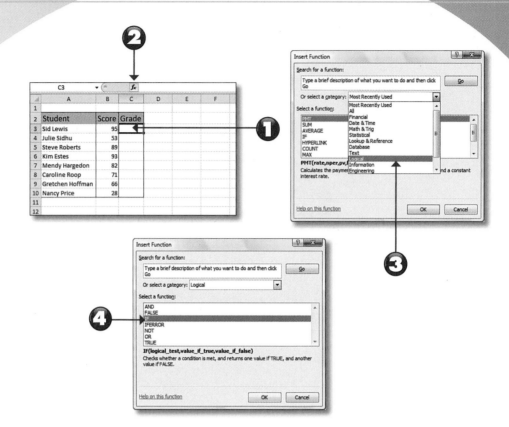

Start

1 Click in the cell in which you want the result of the function to appear (this is called the *resultant cell*).

2 Click the **Insert Function (fx)** command next to the Formula bar.

3 The Insert Function dialog box opens. Click the **down arrow** next to the Or Select a Category field and choose **Logical** from the list that appears.

4 A list of logical functions appears in the Select a Function list. Scroll through the list to locate the IF function and double-click it.

Continued

NOTE

Embedded IFs You can set up embedded IF statements to use in your logical test. For example, suppose scores between 90-100 are an A, 80-89 are a B, 70-79 are a C, 60-69 are a D, and scores below 59 are an F. Your formula might look like this: =IF(B3>89, "A", IF(B3>79, "B", IF(B3>69, "C", IF(B3>59, "D", "F")). ∎

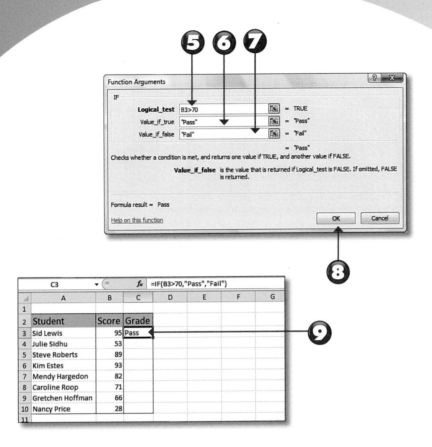

5 In the Logical_test field, type the condition to determine whether a grade is above 70. The logical test is whether the cell is greater than 70; for example, **B3>70**.

6 In the Value_if_true field, type the value you want to use if the grade is above 70 (that is, a passing grade)—for example, **"Pass"**.

7 In the Value_if_false field, type the value you want to use if the grade is below 70 (that is, a failing grade)—for example, **"Fail"**.

8 Click **OK**.

9 Excel performs the logical test and inserts the result in the resultant cell.

End

TIP

Quick Help with Functions   You can press the F1 key on your keyboard any time you're typing up an Excel function to automatically be brought to that Function's help screen. ■

CONDITIONALLY SUMMING A RANGE (SUMIF)

Using Excel, you can add the data in a range, given certain criteria. This might be useful if, for instance, you need to total the current monthly sales for all sales reps who match a specific criterion—for example, who are all in the same sales region.

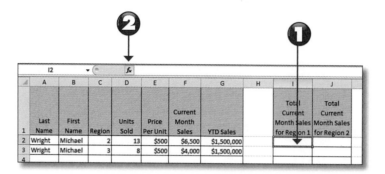

Start

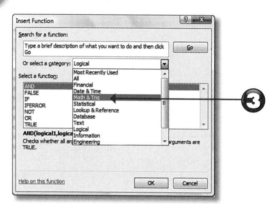

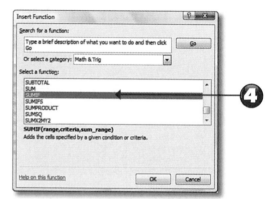

1. Click in the cell in which you want the result of the function to appear (this is called the *resultant cell*).

2. Click the **Insert Function (fx)** command next to the Formula bar.

3. The Insert Function dialog box opens. Click the **down arrow** next to the Or Select a Category field and choose **Math & Trig** from the list that appears.

4. A list of math and trig functions appears in the Select a Function list. Scroll through the list to locate the SUMIF function and double-click it.

Continued

NOTE

Function Arguments Help   If you need help while you are entering your function arguments, click the Help On This Function link in the bottom-left corner of the Function Arguments dialog box. ■

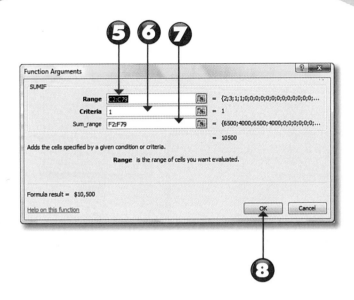

5 In the Range field, type the range of cells whose contents you want to review—for example, **C2:C79**. (You can also click directly in the worksheet to select the cells.)

6 In the Criteria field, type the criterion you want to check in the range—in this case, type **"1"** because you want to add sales data from Region 1 only.

7 In the Sum_range field, type the range of cells that match your criterion—in this case, **F2:F79**, which contains the current month sales data.

8 Click **OK**.

9 Excel adds the range given your criteria and inserts the result in the resultant cell.

End

NOTE

Range Selection In addition to typing specific Range and Sum_range arguments, you can click in the worksheet and select each range of cells using the mouse. ▪

FINDING THE FUTURE VALUE OF AN INVESTMENT (FV)

If you open a 3% interest-bearing money market account with $100 in January and make deposits of $100 each month, how much money will you have at the end of the year? Excel can help you calculate the future value of an amount of money, based on a constant interest rate, over a specific number of periods in which you make a constant payment.

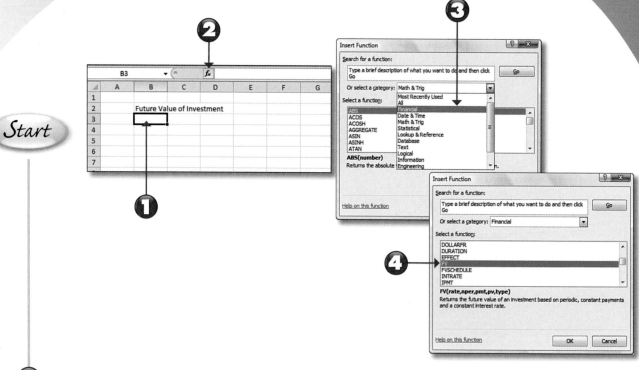

Start

① Click in the cell in which you want the result of the function to appear (this is called the *resultant cell*).

② Click the **Insert Function (fx)** command next to the Formula bar.

③ The Insert Function dialog box opens. Click the **down arrow** next to the Or Select a Category field and choose **Financial** from the list that appears.

④ A list of financial-related functions appears in the Select a Function list. Scroll through the list to locate the FV function and double-click it.

Continued

NOTE

Function arguments help If you need help while you are inputting your function arguments, click the Help on this function link in the bottom-left corner of the Function Arguments dialog box. ■

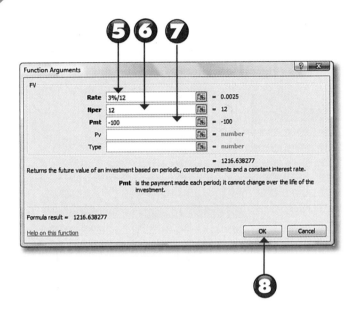

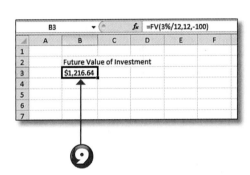

5 In the Rate field, type the interest rate per period. For example, type **3%/12** for monthly accrual on a 3% interest-bearing account.

6 In the Nper field, type the total number of payments for the investment (in this example, **12** deposits).

7 In the Pmt field, type the amount to be paid in each deposit—in this case, **-100**.

8 Click **OK**.

9 Excel calculates the future investment value and inserts it in the resultant cell.

End

NOTE

Negative Payments   Because you are making a payment with each deposit, you need to make sure the Pmt argument is a negative value. ■

FIXING THE #### ERROR

Excel notifies you when there are errors in your data by displaying different error descriptions in the cell that contains the error. For example, when a cell contains the value ####, it means that the column that contains that value is not wide enough to display the actual data. Simply widen the column to see the cell's contents.

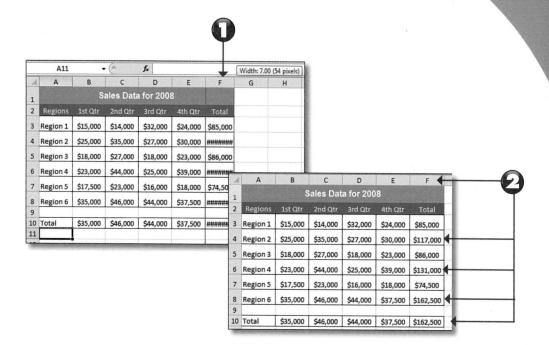

Start

1 If one of the cells in your worksheet contains the #### error, click on the cell's column border and drag it to increase the column width.

2 When you let go of the dragged border, the error disappears and the cell's actual data is displayed.

End

NOTE

Beginning with Larger Columns It is a good idea to start out with columns that are larger than you need. Then you can decrease their size while you are formatting the worksheet. ■

NOTE

AutoFitting Column Widths To automatically make an entire column (or multiple columns) fit the width of the widest cell in that column (or columns), move the cursor over the right side of the column header and double-click when the cursor changes to a two-headed arrow. ■

FIXING THE #DIV/o! ERROR

Excel notifies you when there are errors in your data by displaying different error descriptions in the cell that contains the error. For example, when a cell contains the #DIV/O! error, it means that the formula is trying to divide a number by 0, or by an empty cell.

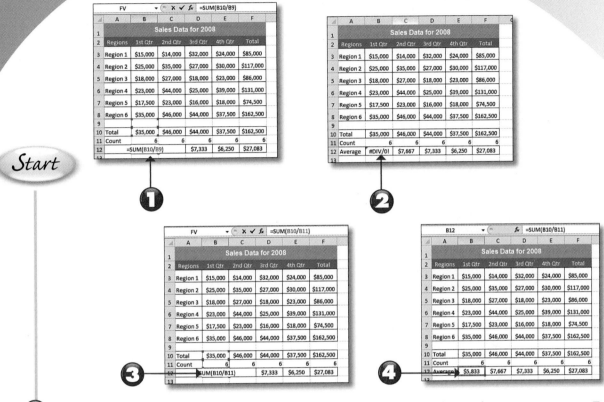

Start

1 In the cell you want to use as the resultant cell, type a formula to obtain an average. For example, type **=SUM(B10/B9)** in cell B12 and press **Enter**.

2 If one of the cells in your worksheet now contains the #DIV/O! error, locate the empty cell referenced by the formula (in this case, cell B9).

3 Click on the resultant cell (here, B12), press **F2** on the keyboard, and retype the formula to omit the empty cell—in this case, **=(B10/B11)**—and press **Enter**.

4 The error disappears because it is no longer trying to divide a number by an empty cell.

End

NOTE

Pressing the Delete Key   In this example, you could also press the Delete key in cell B9 to remove the formula. ■

FIXING THE #NAME? ERROR

Excel notifies you when there are errors in your data by displaying different error descriptions in the cell that contains the error. For example, when a cell contains a #NAME? error, it means the formula contains an incorrectly spelled cell or function name.

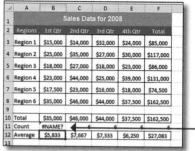

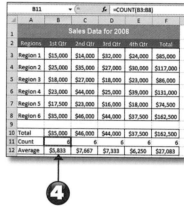

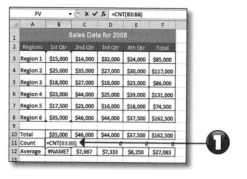

Start

1. In the cell you want to use as the resultant cell, type the formula you want to use in your calculation. For example, type **=CNT(B3:B8)** in cell B11 and press **Enter**.

2. In this case, you get the #NAME? error because CNT is not the correct spelling for the referenced function (it is COUNT).

3. Click on the resultant cell (here, B11), press **F2** on the keyboard, and retype the formula—in this case, **=COUNT(B3:B8)**—and press **Enter**.

4. The error disappears because the function is spelled correctly.

End

NOTE

Using the Paste Function Dialog Box The Paste Function dialog box offers many functions. Practice using different functions and see the results you get from your calculations. As you experiment, you can move the Paste Function dialog box around or collapse it to see your cells. ∎

FIXING THE #VALUE! ERROR

Excel notifies you when there are errors in your data by displaying different error descriptions in the cell that contains the error. For example, when a cell contains a #VALUE! value, it means the formula contains nonnumeric data or cell or function names that cannot be used in the calculation.

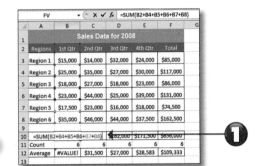

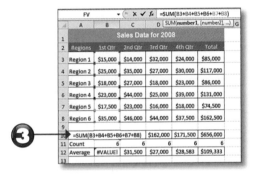

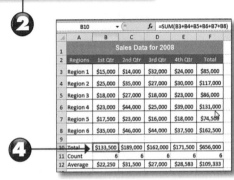

Start

1 In the cell you want to use as the resultant cell, type the formula you want to use in your calculation. For example, type **=SUM(B2+B3+B4+B5+B6+B7+B8)** in cell B10, and press **Enter**.

2 In this case, you get the #VALUE! error because the value in cell B2 is textual, not numeric. You won't get the error if you either remove B2 or you replace the formula with =SUM(B2:B5) instead of the plus signs.

3 Click on the resultant cell (here, B10), press **F2** on the keyboard, and retype the formula—in this case, **=SUM(B3+B4+B5+B6+B7+B8)**—and press **Enter**.

4 The error disappears because all cells are now numeric.

End

NOTE

Overwriting Cells See the task "Overwriting and Deleting Data" in Chapter 3, "Entering and Managing Data," to make sure you are correctly overwriting data in cells. ∎

RECOGNIZING THE #REF! ERROR

Excel notifies you when there are errors in your data by displaying different error descriptions in the cell that contains the error. For example, when a cell contains a #REF! error, it means the formula contains a reference to a cell that isn't valid. Frequently, this means you deleted a referenced cell. The best solution is to undo your action and review the cells involved in the formula.

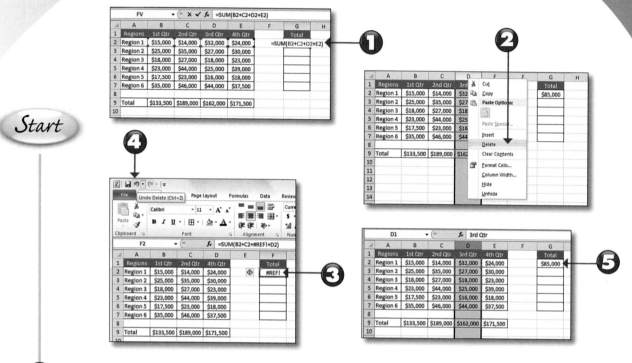

Start

1. In the cell you want to use as the resultant cell, type the formula you want to use in your calculation. For example, type **=SUM(B2+C2+D2+E2)** and press **Enter**.

2. Right-click one of the columns that contains a cell referenced in the formula you just typed (here, column D), and choose **Delete** from the shortcut menu that appears.

3. In this case, the #REF! error appears because the values in cells referenced in column D are no longer available in the formula.

4. Click the **Undo** command to correct it.

5. The error disappears because the formula values are restored.

End

RECOGNIZING CIRCULAR REFERENCES

Excel notifies you when there are errors in your data by displaying different error descriptions in the cell that contains the error. For example, you receive a circular reference error message when one of the cells you are referencing in your calculation is the cell in which you want the calculation to appear.

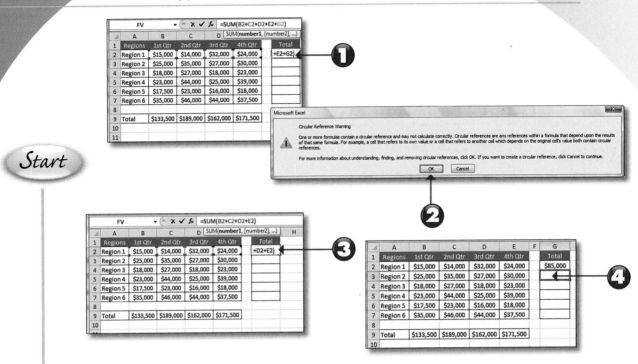

Start

1 Type the formula you want to use in your calculation. For example, type **=SUM(B2+C2+D2+E2+G2)** and press **Enter**.

2 Excel displays an error message, notifying you that the formula contains a circular reference. Click **OK**.

3 Click on the resultant cell, press **F2** on the keyboard, and retype your formula—in this case, **=SUM(B2+C2+D2+E2)**—and press **Enter**.

4 The error is fixed because the result cell no longer is in the calculation.

End

NOTE

Circular Reference Dialog If you didn't intend to create a circular reference and you chose OK in the message box, the Circular Reference dialog and Help will appear to assist you in correcting your actions. ■

CHECKING FOR FORMULA REFERENCES (PRECEDENTS)

One way to check a formula to see whether it is referencing the correct cells is to select that formula and then trace all cells that are referenced in that formula. Cells that are referenced are called *precedents*.

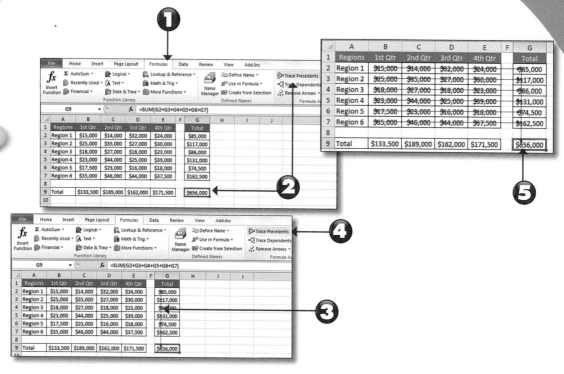

Start

1 Click on the **Formulas** tab.

2 Click the cell you want to trace (this cell must contain a formula) and click the **Trace Precedents** command.

3 Excel draws tracer arrows to the appropriate cells.

4 Click the **Trace Precedents** command again to see whether there are any precedents for these calculations.

5 If additional precedents are present, Excel draws additional tracer arrows to the cells.

End

NOTE

Removing Formula Auditing Lines References Click the Remove Precedents Arrows command on the Formula tab to remove the arrows. ■

CHECKING FOR CELL REFERENCES (DEPENDENTS)

When you trace a dependent, you start with a cell that is referenced in a formula and then trace all cells that reference this cell. This is another way to check whether your formulas are correct. (If the cell is not referenced in a formula, you get an error message saying so.)

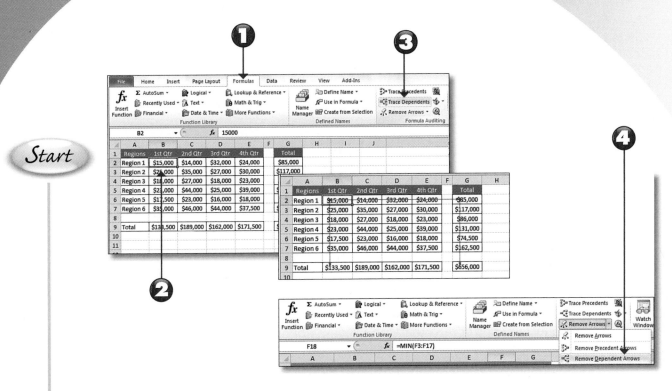

Start

1. Click on the **Formulas** tab.

2. Click the cell you want to trace. This cell must not contain a formula.

3. Click the **Trace Dependents** command until the tracer arrows stop adding on to the appropriate cells.

4. Click the **Remove Dependent Arrows** command enough times to remove all the arrows (or click the **Remove All Arrows** command).

End

NOTE

Using Trace Errors   If the cell contains an error message, use the Trace Errors command to have Excel trace possible reasons for the error. ■

Chapter 6

WORKING WITH CHARTS

Charts are graphical representations of data that allow you to visualize and communicate your data in a more meaningful way than with simple numbers in tables. In Excel, you not only have the capability to easily chart your data, but you can also quickly change the appearance of charts with a bevy of options. For instance, you can change titles, customize the legend, set axis points, add category names, and more.

As mentioned in Chapter 1, "Working with the Excel User Interface," certain Excel objects activate **contextual tabs** in Excel 2010. These contextual tabs are special types of tabs that appear only when a particular object is selected. When you work with Excel charts, you see the Chart Tools contextual tab. This tab contains sub-tabs that expose the various commands you would use to design, layout, and format a chart.

In this chapter, you will discover just how easy it is to create charts in Excel.

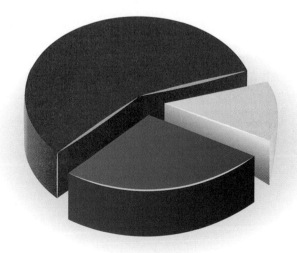

THE CHART TOOLS CONTEXTUAL TAB

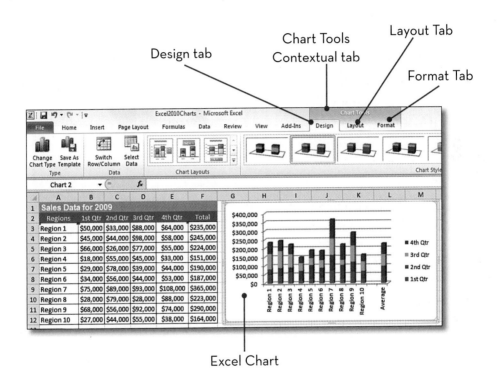

Design tab

Chart Tools Contextual tab

Layout Tab

Format Tab

Excel Chart

CREATING A CHART

Interpreting numeric data by looking at numbers in a table can be difficult. Using data to create charts can help people visualize the data's significance. For example, you might not have noticed in a spreadsheet that the same month of every year has low sales figures, but it becomes obvious when you make a chart from the data in that spreadsheet. The chart's visual nature also helps others review your data without the need to review every single number.

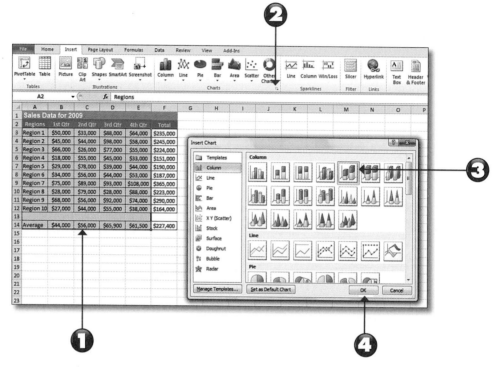

Start

1. Select the cells you want to include in your chart.

2. Click the **Create Chart** dialog launcher at the bottom right-hand corner of the Charts group on the Ribbon's Insert tab.

3. Click on the **Chart Type** icon for the chart you want to create.

4. Click the **OK** button to create your chart.

Continued

NOTE

Creating Quick Charts   You can quickly create a chart by selecting your data range and pressing the F11 key on your keyboard. When you do this, Excel automatically creates a chart and puts it on its own tab. ■

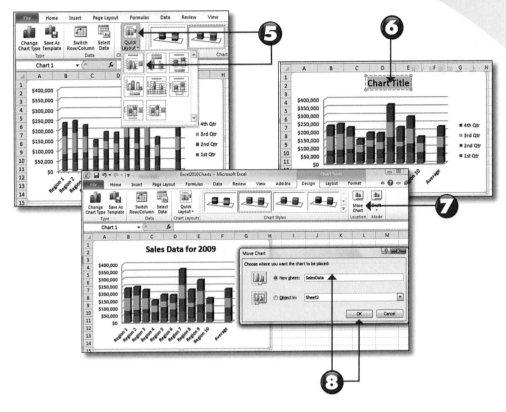

5 On the Design tab, you see the Chart Layouts group. There, you can click the Quick Layout command to choose a chart layout that includes a chart title.

6 Click the **Chart Title** box and then type the name for the chart.

7 Click the **Move Chart** option button on the Design tab.

8 Enter the name you want for the new worksheet and then click **OK**. In this case, Excel moves the chart to a new worksheet named SalesData.

End

NOTE

Moving a Chart Regardless of your selection in step 6, you can always move your chart to another (perhaps new) worksheet. Simply right-click a blank area in the chart and click Move Chart. To place the chart in a new worksheet, click the **New sheet** option and type a name for the new sheet. To move it to a different worksheet, click the **Object in** option button and select the worksheet from the drop-down list. Click OK, and Excel moves the chart. ∎

CHANGING THE CHART TYPE

Charting is one of those skills you learn by doing. At first, you might not even know what type of chart you want to create until you see it. You can always select a different chart type for a chart so that it better represents the data.

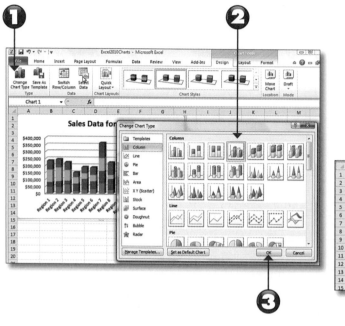

 Click the **Change Chart Type** command on the Design tab.

2 Select a new chart type and chart subtype in the Chart Type dialog box.

3 Click **OK**.

4 The updated chart type appears in your chart.

Start

End

NOTE

Using the Default Chart Type The default chart type is a column chart. To make another chart type the default, select it in the Change Chart Type dialog box and then click the Set As Default Chart button. ■

ALTERING THE SOURCE DATA RANGE

Suppose you need to point your chart to a completely different data table. That is, the data that feeds your chart will be coming from a different location. In this scenario, you can reconfigure your chart to change its source data location.

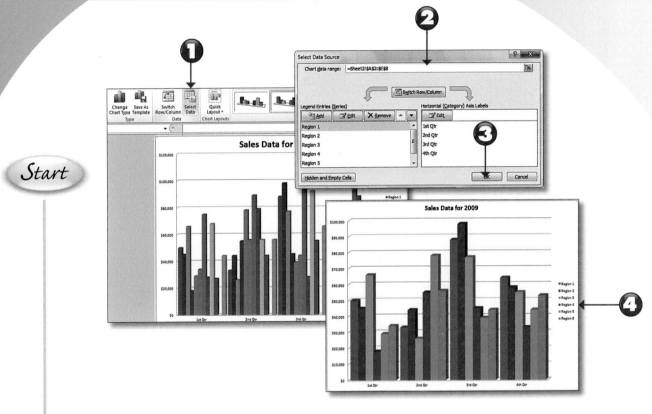

Start

① Go to the Design tab and select the **Select Data** command.

② Click directly in your worksheet and select the new data range. The Data range area in the Source Data dialog box automatically updates.

③ Click **OK**.

④ The updated data range appears in your chart.

End

NOTE

Locating Incorrect Data If you notice that one of the data points in your chart is way off the scale, this is a good sign that you might have entered data into your worksheet incorrectly. If this is the case, edit the worksheet data and the chart updates automatically. (See the task "Changing the Chart Source Data" later in this chapter for help altering the original data. ■

ALTERING CHART OPTIONS

Changing your chart options is even easier than creating the chart in the first place. You can add or edit chart titles, alter your axes, add or remove gridlines, move or delete your legend, add or remove data labels, and even show the data table containing your original data. All of this can be managed from the Layout tab.

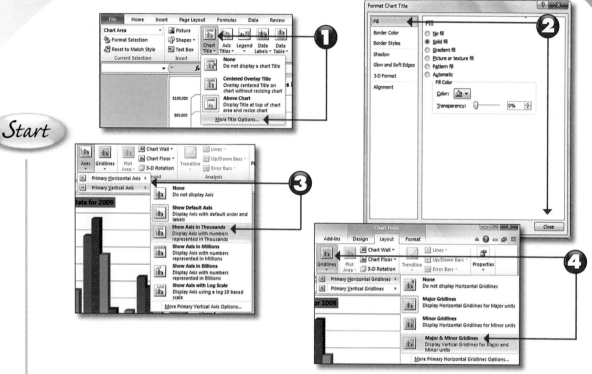

 Start

1 Click the **Chart Title** button and choose **More Title Options**.

2 In the Fill section, add a background color by checking **Solid Fill** and then click **Close**.

3 Click the **Axes** button and then select **Primary Vertical Axis**, **Show Axis in Thousands** to change the format of the vertical axis.

4 Click the **Gridlines** button and then select **Primary Horizontal Gridlines, Major & Minor Gridlines** to make both visible on the chart.

Continued

NOTE

Formatting the Axes Gridlines   To change the pattern and scale of the gridlines, double-click the gridline itself and then use the Format Gridlines dialog box to make your selections. Click **OK** when finished. ∎

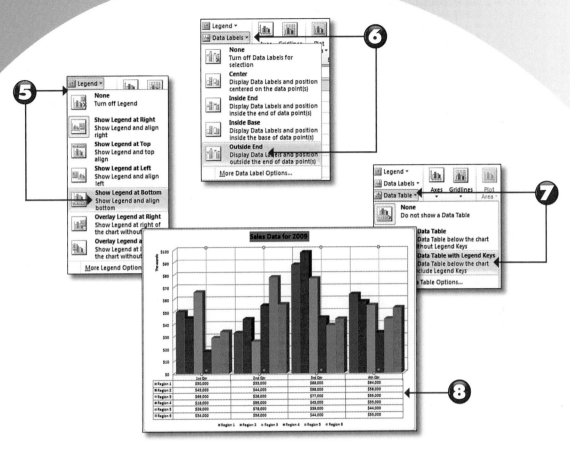

5 Click the **Legend** tab, select whether you want to show a legend, and review how altering the Placement options affects your chart.

6 Click the **Data Labels** tab and see how the addition of label descriptions affects your chart.

7 Click the **Data Table** tab and select whether you want to show the data table (with or without the legend keys).

8 Review how your chart has changed.

End

TIP

Adding Data Tables If you want to show a data table along with the chart, go to the Layout tab and click Data Table, Show Data Table.

NOTE

Printing Charts f you want to print just your chart (as opposed to the entire worksheet) select the chart and click the Print Selected Chart option under the Print pane of the Backstage view. ■

FORMATTING THE PLOT AREA

The *plot area* consists of a border and the location of the data points in your chart. You can alter the style, color, and weight of the border. You can also alter the color of the plot area.

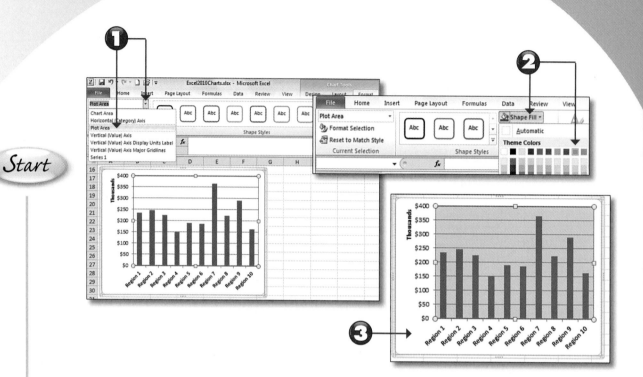

Start

End

1. Go to the Format tab and click on the Chart Elements **drop-down**, then choose **Plot Area** from the drop-down.

2. Click on the **Shape Fill** button and choose a color to change the background color of the plot area.

3. Observe how your chart has changed.

TIP

Determining which Area You're In   If you are unsure whether you are in the chart area or the plot area, click directly on the chart. Look at the Chart Elements drop-down found in the upper-left corner of the Format tab. This drop-down shows the name of the chart element that is currently active. You can also use this nifty drop-down to quickly switch from one element to another. ■

FORMATTING THE CHART AREA

The *chart area* consists of a border, the background, and all the chart fonts. You can alter the style, color, and weight of the border. You can also alter the color of the background. You can also change all the fonts and font styles in the chart.

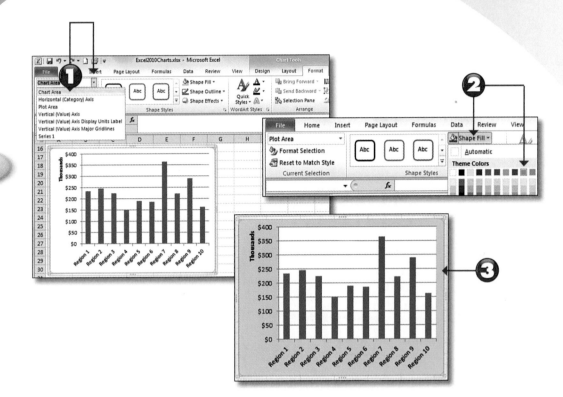

Start

1 Go to the Format tab and click on the Chart Elements **drop-down**, then choose **Chart Area** from the drop-down.

2 Click on the **Shape Fill** button and then choose a color to change the background color of the plot area.

3 Observe how your chart has changed.

End

TIP

Formatting from the Home Tab You can change the font and color of most chart elements by using the formatting commands on the Home tab. You can simply select the chart element and use the Home tab to easily change the font, alignment, color, and other format properties. This makes quick work of any formatting tasks you may need to do on your charts. ■

FORMATTING THE AXIS SCALE

Excel automatically establishes the axis increments according to the maximum amount on the chart. Usually this will suffice, but if you want to show more detail about actual numbers, it can be convenient to alter your value axis.

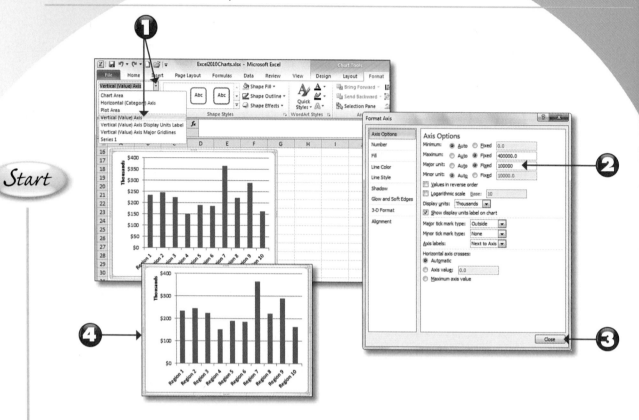

Start

End

1 Go to the Format tab and click on the Chart Elements **drop-down**, then choose **Vertical (Value) Axis** from the drop-down.

2 Click the **Scale** tab of the Format Axis dialog box and type the changes to the axis scale increments—for example, decrease the value in the Major unit field.

3 Click **Close**.

4 Review how your chart has changed.

NOTE

Number and Alignment To change the number format, click the Number tab and select the numeric format you want to use. To change the alignment, click the Alignment tab and select a rotation for the axes. ■

ALTERING THE ORIGINAL DATA

A chart is linked to the worksheet data, so when you make a change in the worksheet, the chart is updated. If you want to change a value in the worksheet, edit it as you do normally. The chart is instantly updated to reflect the change. If you delete data in the worksheet, the matching data series is deleted in the chart.

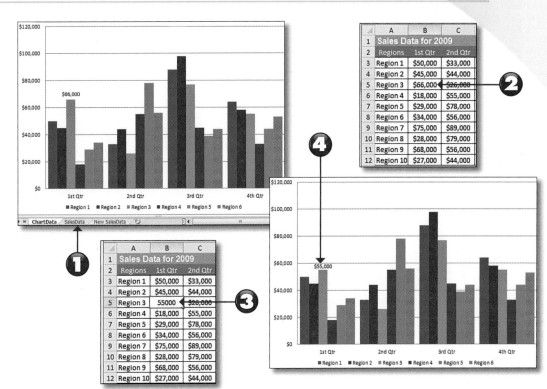

Start

1 Select the worksheet tab or range that contains the charted data.

2 Click a cell that you want to alter or need to update.

3 Type in the new data and press the **Enter** key.

4 Go back to the chart and see how the edited data point has changed your chart.

End

TIP

Saving Changes   When working with charts, you want to make sure you save your changes often. You wouldn't want to lose any changes you made in case your network goes down or your computer freezes. ■

ADDING DATA TO CHARTS

Suppose you want to expand your chart to include additional data. If so, you need to place the data on your original worksheet and indicate to Excel that you want it included in your chart.

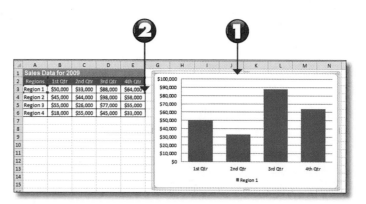

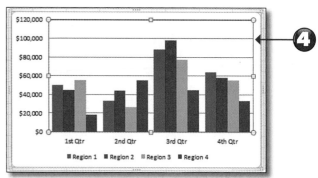

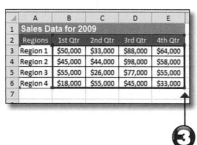

Start

End

1 After adding any new data you want to include in your chart to the original data range, click directly on your chart to see what data is currently referenced in the chart.

2 Click and drag the blue chart data line to include the newly added data.

3 Use the blue handle to drag the chart data line in the new location.

4 The chart automatically updates to include the new data.

NOTE

Excluding Chart Data   You can also click and drag the blue chart data line to exclude data in your chart. Simply drag the blue line so that the data you want to exclude is no longer contained within the chart. ■

ADDING A LEGEND

A *legend* helps a reader make sense of all the data points and colors shown in a chart. You typically wouldn't need a legend if you're plotting only one data series. However, if you are plotting two or more data series in one chart, it's definitely a best practice to have a legend. Considering the fact that you will probably add data to your chart, going from one data series to many, it's helpful to know how to add a legend after your chart has been created.

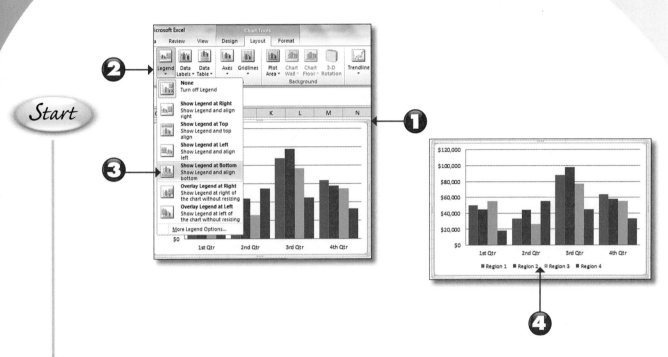

Start

End

1. Click anywhere on your chart.

2. Go to the Layout tab and Click the **Legend** command.

3. Select the **Show Legend at Bottom** option.

4. Note that your chart now has a Legend.

TIP

Formatting Legends   Right-click the legend and choose Format Legend from the shortcut menu. From the dialog box that appears, you can alter the patterns, fonts, and even the placement of the legend. ■

Chapter 7

WORKING WITH GRAPHICS

There might be instances when you're asked to add graphics to your Excel worksheets. For example, you might need to insert your company's logo on each worksheet you create. Well, the good news is that Excel has a whole host of tools that enable you to create and customize your own graphics and visualizations. With these tools, you can add a picture from another file, draw pictures, insert shapes, use ClipArt, and create your own WordArt.

In this chapter, you discover the ins and outs of creating and customizing your own Graphics in Excel.

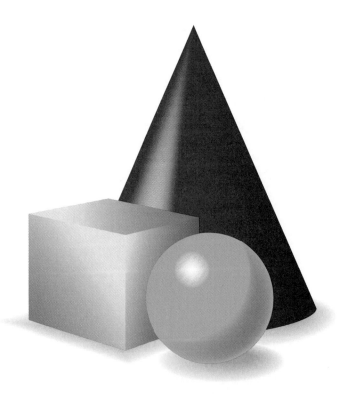

INSERTED GRAPHIC OBJECTS

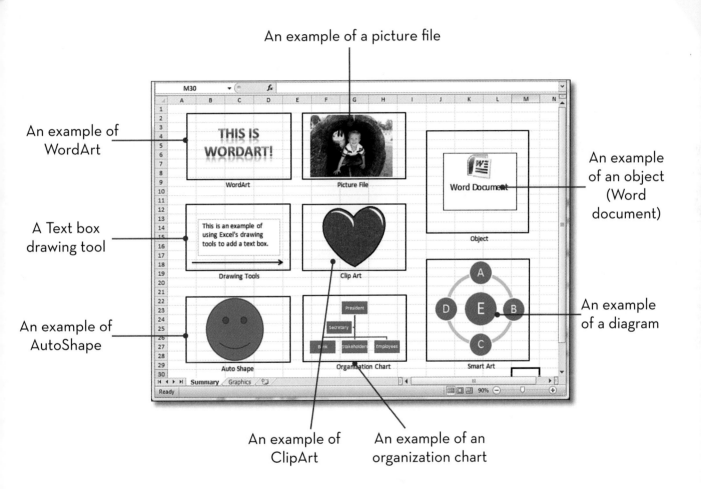

An example of a picture file

An example of WordArt

An example of an object (Word document)

A Text box drawing tool

An example of AutoShape

An example of a diagram

An example of ClipArt

An example of an organization chart

USING DRAWING TOOLS

Excel has drawing tools that you can use to draw on a worksheet or chart. In this task, you learn about the advantages of using Excel drawing tools to point out information on a worksheet.

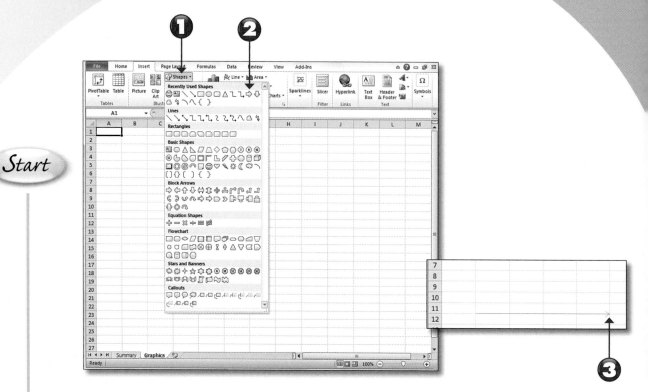

 Start

1 On the Insert tab, Click the **Shapes** drop-down.

2 Click any of the drawing tools' buttons—for example, the Arrow. The mouse pointer turns into a plus sign.

3 Click and drag in the worksheet to draw an arrow; release the mouse button when the arrow is the length you want it to be. (The pointer end will be at the point of release.)

Continued

NOTE

Quick Color and Style If you click on any shape, you will see a new Drawing Tools Format tab. There, you can apply some predefined styles for your shapes by choosing a style from the Shape Styles gallery. ■

TIP

Using AutoShapes You'll notice that the Shapes Command (on the Insert tab) includes tools for drawing common shapes, such as lines, circles, squares, and so on. If you aren't much of an artist or if you want to try some prefab symbols, insert an AutoShape. You can select from several lines, connectors, basic shapes, arrows, flowchart symbols, stars, callouts, banners, and more. ■

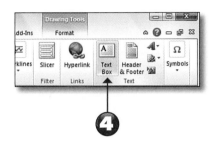

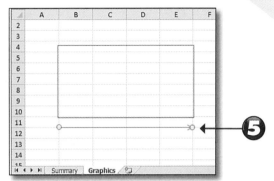

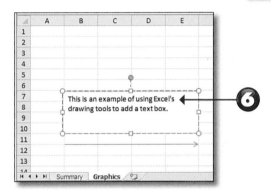

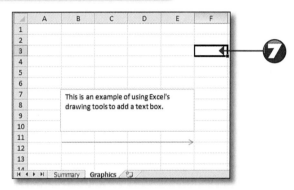

 As another example, click the **Text Box** command on the Insert tab. The mouse pointer turns into an insertion pointer.

5 Click and drag in the worksheet to draw a text box; release the mouse button when the box is the size you want it to be.

6 Type the text you want to enter in the text box.

7 Click anywhere outside the text box to see how it looks.

End

NOTE

Text Boxes   Use text boxes to move, resize, and format them. This is an excellent alternative to formatting a cell in a worksheet where real estate can be limited. ■

TIP

Modifying Drawing Objects   A drawn object is like a picture—you can edit it as needed. To resize a drawn object, click the object; then drag the sizing handles to the size you want and release the mouse button. To move the object, click the object and drag it to the desired location. ■

INSERTING CLIP ART

Clip art adds visual interest to your Excel worksheets. With Microsoft clip art, you can choose from numerous professionally prepared images, sounds, and movie clips. After you add graphics, you can move them around in the worksheet and even assign text wrapping.

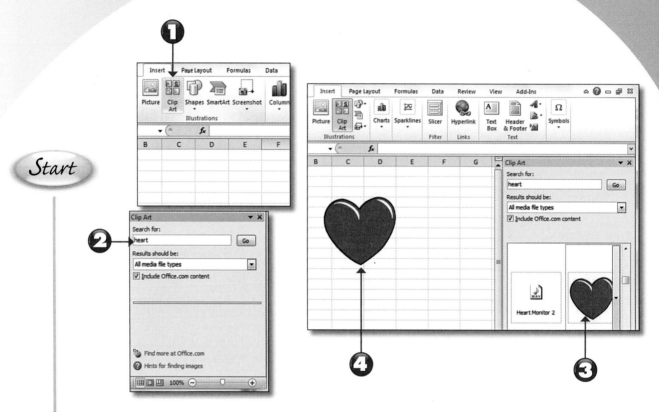

Start

1. Click the **Clip Art** button on the Insert tab to open the Clip Art task pane.

2. Type a description for the clip art you are looking for in the Search for Text box, and press **Enter** (or click the Go button).

3. If Microsoft has clip art that matches the description you type, it displays in the Clip Art task pane. Click an image in the results list to insert it into your worksheet.

4. The clip art is inserted into your worksheet. (You might need to move or resize the image; see the tasks "Moving an Object" and "Resizing an Object.")

End

TIP

The Picture Tools Format Tab If you click on any picture or clip art, you will see a new Picture Tools Format tab. There, you will find tools to crop, format, adjust contrast, apply effects, and most anything else you would typically do to a picture. ■

INSERTING A PICTURE FROM FILE

Often times, you will want to embed your own company-approved pictures into your worksheet. A good example of this is a company logo. Excel is quite flexible and allows you to insert varying types of picture files: Bitmap files, JPEG files, PNG Files, TIF files, PCX files, and many more.

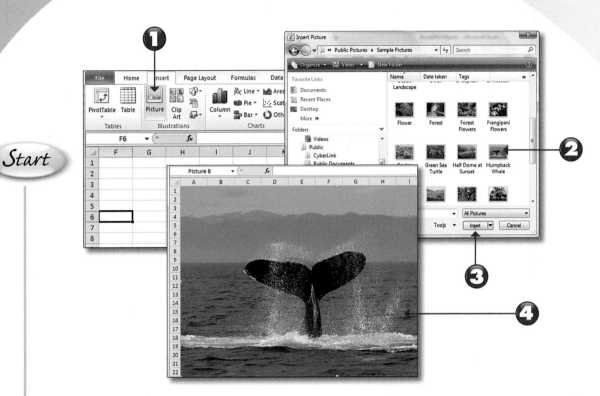

1 On the Insert tab, click the **Picture** button to open the Insert Picture dialog box.

2 Locate the file you want to use, and click it to see a preview. (You might need to select **Preview** from the dialog box Views button).

3 Click the **Insert** button.

4 The image is inserted into your worksheet.

TIP

Manage Overlapping Picture Objects If you have multiple pictures on your worksheet, you can manage how the pictures overlap each other. Right-click on each picture and select either Send to Back or Bring to Front. This way, you can better control the layout of your pictures, and even layer your pictures to create robust visualizations. ■

USING AUTOSHAPES

Excel enables you to add numerous predesigned shapes, called AutoShapes, to your worksheets. For example, you can insert any one of the following AutoShapes into your worksheet: Lines, Connectors, Basic Shapes, Block Arrows, Flowchart, Stars and Banners, Callouts, and more. AutoShapes are ideal when you don't want to spend the time to draw your own fancy symbols, instead preferring to get up and running with one of Excel's prefab symbols.

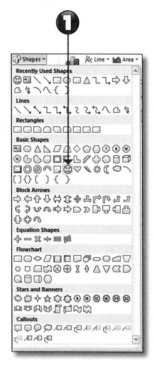

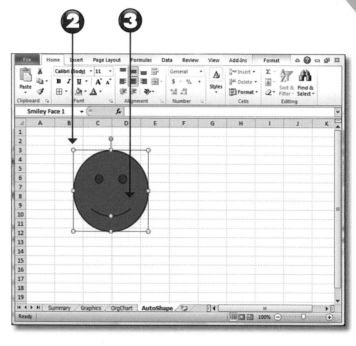

Start

On the Insert tab, click the **Shapes** drop-down, and select from the different shape options (here, Smiley Face).

The mouse pointer changes to a plus sign. Click and drag the pointer to draw the object at the desired size; then release the mouse button.

The new shape is added, complete with sizing handles.

End

NOTE

Resizing and Moving Objects   Move the mouse over an object border; the pointer becomes a four-headed arrow, and you can move it (see the "Moving Objects" task); a two-headed arrow enables you to resize it (see the "Resizing Objects" task). ■

NOTE

Formatting AutoShapes   To format your AutoShape, right-click the object, and select Format Shape from the shortcut menu. Click the Colors and Lines tab, and choose from the various colors, line types, and arrows. You can also use the Format tab that appears on the ribbon after you select an Autoshape. ■

INSERTING WORDART

WordArt is a text-based object that Microsoft provides to apply special effects to text. You don't have to add these text effects manually; the different styles of WordArt are indeed the text effects themselves.

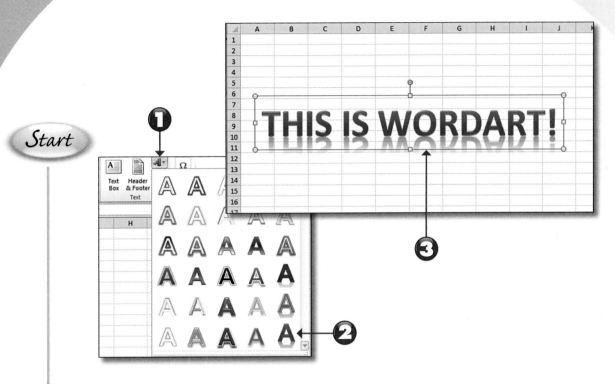

① On the Insert tab, click the **WordArt** button to open the WordArt Gallery.

② Click the WordArt style you want to use to insert it onto the worksheet.

③ Type your text into the Text box placed on the worksheet, and press **Enter**.

End

NOTE

Formatting WordArt After your WordArt is inserted into your worksheet, the Drawing Tools contextual tab appears on the ribbon (while the WordArt object is selected). You can use the Drawing Tools contextual tab to edit the text, alter the style, format the text, and add more WordArt. ■

USING SMART ART IN EXCEL

Smart Art is often described as representation of information and ideas. You can think of Smart Art as a way to visually communicate concepts that are difficult to communicate with data alone. For example, it would be difficult to build a data table that effectively communicates an organizations hierarchy. This is where Smart Art would come in.

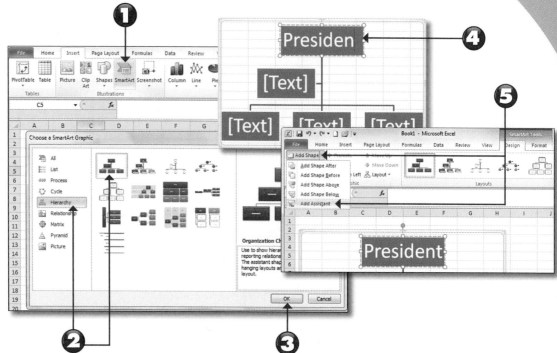

Start

1. On the Insert tab, choose **SmartArt**.

2. Select **Organization Chart** under the Hierarchy pane.

3. Click OK to insert the new Smart Art into your Worksheet.

4. An organization chart containing dummy text is inserted into your worksheet. To fill the chart in yourself, click a text box and type over the dummy text with your own text.

5. The Smart Art Tools tab offers options such as adding a subordinate, co-worker, or assistant, to the selected text box. For example, you can click the dropdown next to the **Add Shape** button and select **Add Assistant**.

End

INSERTING A DIAGRAM

Diagrams are ideal when you need to integrate and communicate a workflow, process, or other conceptual paradigms with your spreadsheet data. You can insert the diagram and then add the appropriate information in a manner similar to inserting an organization chart.

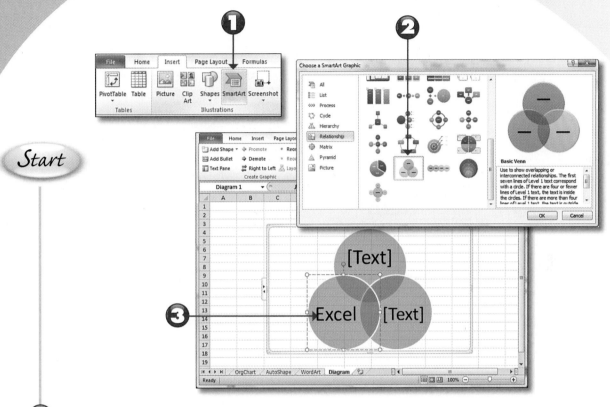

Start

1 On the Insert tab click the **SmartArt** button to display the SmartArt Gallery dialog box.

2 Double-click the desired diagram type; a diagram of that type containing dummy text is inserted into your worksheet.

3 Click each instance of dummy text and type over it with text of your own.

End

TIP

Make Use of the Layout Gallery   After your diagram is in place, use the Layout gallery under the Design tab to try out different layouts. Excel keeps all your text and settings but shows your diagram in a different layout. Often times, you'll find one that better illustrates your message than the one you originally selected. ■

INSERTING AN OBJECT

In addition to inserting all the different types of graphic objects that you learned about in this chapter, you can also insert objects that aren't as commonly added to Excel worksheets. For example, you can insert a media clip, PowerPoint slide, Microsoft Works chart, video clip, and much more.

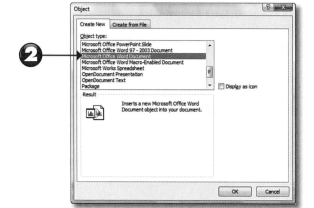

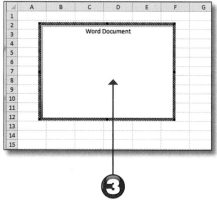

1 On the Insert tab click the **Insert Object** button to open the Object dialog box.

2 Scroll through the Object type list, and double-click the object you want to insert—for example, Microsoft Office Word Document.

3 Edit the object according to the individual object properties (in this example, as you would when creating a Word document).

Start

End

NOTE

Getting to the Object Properties Once your object is on your spreadsheet, you can edit the object by right-clicking it and selecting Document Object. This brings up a Properties menu of sorts. Here, you can Edit the object source, Open the object itself, or convert the object so that it is displayed as an icon. ■

SELECTING AN OBJECT

As you have seen, you can add charts to a worksheet, draw objects, insert pictures, and more. Each of these items exists on a separate layer on top of the worksheet and is generically called an object. As you discover in the next several tasks, you can format, move, resize, and delete objects; first, however, you must select the object you want to modify.

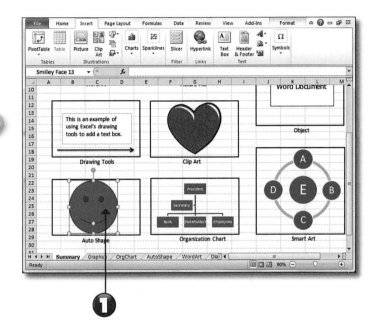

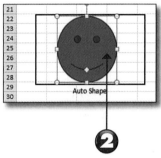

Start

1 Click the object you want to select; selection handles appear around the edges of the object.

2 Move the mouse over the object border; the pointer becomes a four-headed arrow and you can move it; a two-headed arrow enables you to resize it.

End

NOTE

Selecting Multiple Objects To select multiple objects, click the first object, press and hold down the Shift key, and click the second object. Continue until you select all the objects you want. ▪

FORMATTING AN OBJECT

You can format objects just as easily as you format text, data, and worksheets. Depending on the object, the standard formatting options you can change are as follows: font (text changes in the object), alignment (where text aligns in the object), colors and lines (whether lines are filled, colored, or have arrows), size (the height, width, and scale of the object), protection (whether others can alter your object), properties (how you position the object and whether you can print it), and Web (text to display while the object loads online).

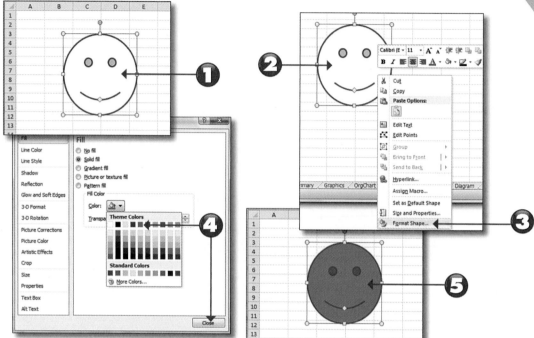

① Click the object you want to format; selection handles appear around the edges of the object.

② Right-click the object.

③ Select **Format** [object name] (here, Shape) from the shortcut menu.

④ A Format [object name] dialog box opens. Click the available tabs, alter the formatting options as needed, and click **Close**.

⑤ The formatting changes are applied to the object.

End

NOTE

Double-Click to the Format Dialog Box You can also double-click directly on the object to automatically open the Format dialog box associated with it. ■

MOVING AN OBJECT

When you draw an object on or add an object to a worksheet, you might not like its placement. Perhaps the object obscures the worksheet data, or maybe it needs to be moved a little closer to (or farther away from) the data. Fortunately, you can easily move an object.

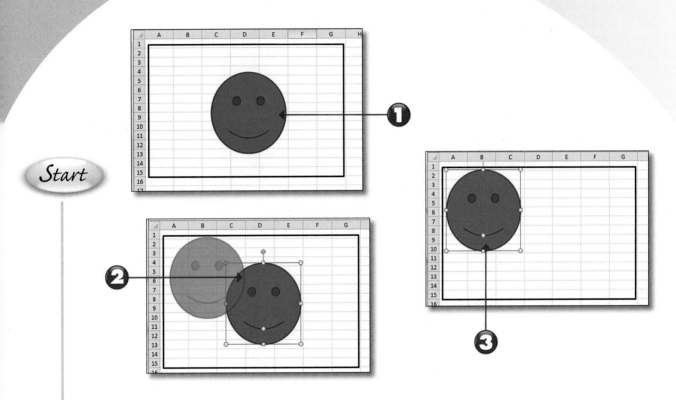

Start

1 Select the object you want to move; selection handles appear around the edges of the object.

2 Click directly on the object or its border (not the selection handles) and hold the left mouse button while dragging the object to the new location.

3 Release the mouse button to drop the object in the new location. The object is moved.

End

TIP

Copying Objects To copy an object, press and hold down the Ctrl key on your keyboard as you drag; a copy of the original object will be moved, with the original remaining intact where it is. ■

NOTE

Moving an Object to Another Worksheet You can move your target object to a separate worksheet by following these simple steps. Right-click the target object, and select Cut. Next, move to the new sheet, right-click in the spot where you want the object to appear, and then select Paste. You can also use these steps to move your object to a different workbook. ■

RESIZING AN OBJECT

If an object is too big (or too small), change the size. You can modify any type of object, including a picture, chart, or drawn object you added. In addition, you can continue to resize the object over and over until it is the size you want.

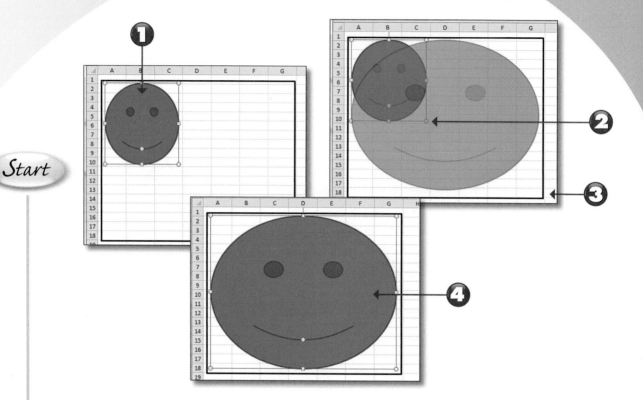

Start

① Select the object you want to resize; selection handles appear around the edges of the object.

② Move the pointer over one of the selection handles (here, a corner handle). When the pointer is in the right spot, it changes to a two-headed arrow.

③ Click the handle, drag it, and release the mouse button when the object is the desired size.

④ The object is resized.

End

NOTE

Corners Versus Sides   Dragging the sides increases or decreases the height or width of an object, whereas dragging the corners increases or decreases the height and width of an object at the same time. ■

NOTE

Resizing Proportionally   If you hold the Shift key down while dragging a corner, the image enlarges or decreases in proportion. ■

DELETING AN OBJECT

As you experiment with charts, drawings, and pictures, you might go overboard, or you might make a mistake and want to start over. In any case, if you add an object and no longer want to include it, you can delete it, as described here.

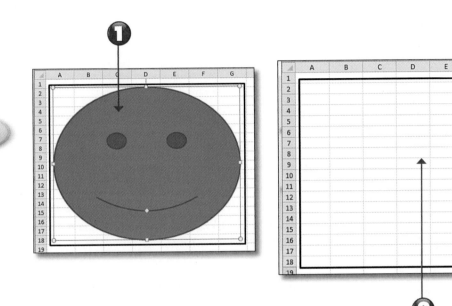

Start

1 Select the object you want to delete; selection handles appear around the edges of the object.

2 Press the **Delete** key on your keyboard. Excel deletes the object.

End

NOTE

Undoing a Deletion   If you accidentally delete an object , click the Undo button on the Quick Access Toolbar to undo the deletion. Alternatively, you can use the Ctrl+Z shortcut on your keyboard. ▪

Chapter 8

PRINTING IN EXCEL

Printing options in Excel 2010 haven't changed that much since Excel 2003. However, it would be foolish not to mention that Excel 2010 does consolidate most printing options into the Backstage View. You can get to the Backstage View by clicking on the File tab on the Ribbon. Although there are several methods of getting to print options, the Excel 2010's Backstage View provides an easy way to quickly configure Excel's print options.

And as you will see, Excel does have a plethora of print options. Don't worry— Excel does allow you to print your worksheets by using basic print settings if that's all you need. But Excel also offers a bevy of settings that enable you to enhance your printouts. Some of these options include orientation adjustments, scaling, paper size options, page numbering, adding headers, adding footers, and more.

In this chapter, you get a tour of the printing options available to you.

PRINT OPTIONS VIA THE BACKSTAGE VIEW

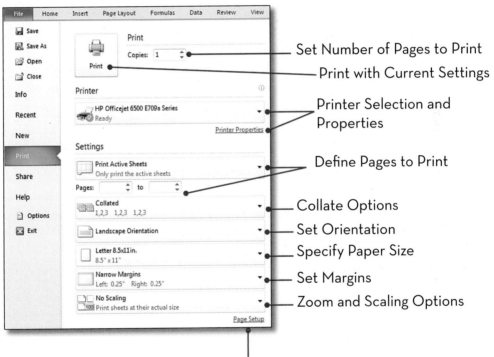

Set Number of Pages to Print

Print with Current Settings

Printer Selection and Properties

Define Pages to Print

Collate Options

Set Orientation

Specify Paper Size

Set Margins

Zoom and Scaling Options

Launch Page Setup Dialog Box

USING PRINT PREVIEW

Worksheets with lots of data can generate large print jobs, possibly containing hundreds of pages. Waiting until all these pages are printed to verify that the information is printed correctly can cost a lot in both time and printing supplies. To help prevent printing mistakes, use Print Preview to ensure that all the necessary elements appear on the pages before printing.

Start

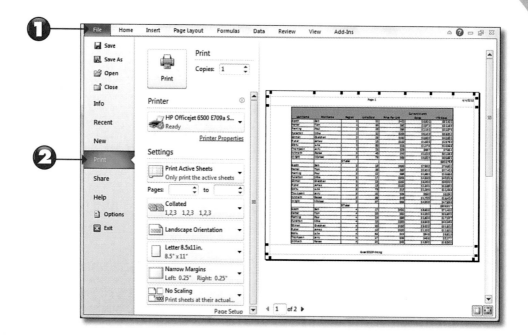

1 With the worksheet you want to print open, click the **File** tab on the ribbon.

2 Click **Print** to display the worksheet's Print Preview.

Continued

NOTE

Paging Through the Print Preview   Note the navigation spinner in the lower left-hand corner of the Print Preview. In this case, the navigation spinner reads 1 of 2. You not only can use this to determine how many pages will be printed, but you can cycle through the pages by clicking the left and right arrows. ■

TIP

Page Break Preview Button   Click Page Break Preview on the View Tab to see and modify exactly what is selected to print (in the print area). If you haven't set the print area, see "Setting the Print Area." ■

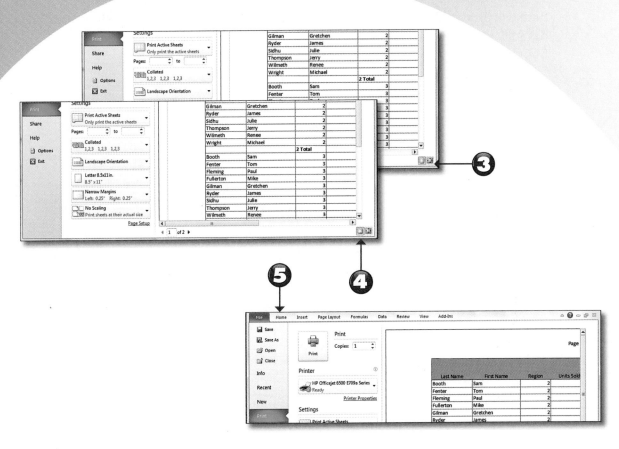

3 Click the **Zoom** button to increase the viewable size of the worksheet in Print Preview mode. (Click Zoom again to return to the original page size.)

4 Click **Margins** to toggle between displaying the margin indicators, which you can drag to set more or less of your worksheet to print.

5 Click the **Home** tab to return to the worksheet's Normal view.

End

TIP

Zoom with your Mouse Wheel You can also use your mouse wheel to zoom in and out of a print preview. Hold down the Ctrl key on your keyboard while you spin your mouse wheel. This increases or reduces magnification of your Print Preview depending on the direction you spin (up or down). ■

SETTING THE PRINT AREA

Worksheets can include several rows and columns; setting the print area enables you to specify which rows and columns to print. If you don't set a print area, all cells that contain data will print. The worksheet in this task contains four tables that span seven pages. By default, all will print unless you set a print area.

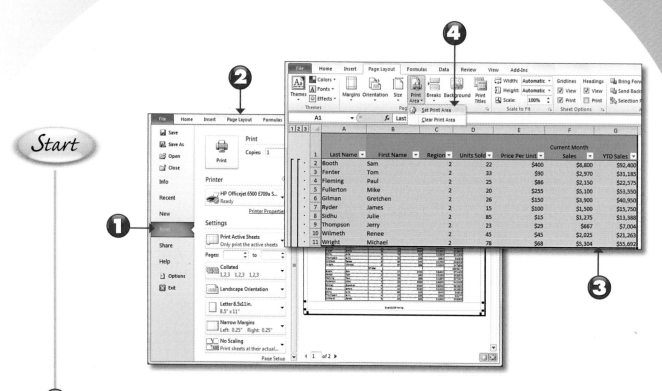

1 Click the **File** tab, then select **Print** to see a Print Preview of your worksheet.

2 Should your print area need adjusting, click on the **Page Layout** menu option to return to Normal view.

3 Select the exact cells you want to print (in this example, all the cells in the first two tables in this worksheet).

4 Click the **Print Area** command on the ribbon, and select **Set Print Area**. This will store the print area as part of the worksheet. Now, only the cells in the print area will print.

End

TIP

Another Way to Choose the Print Area   You can also Set the Print Area from the traditional Page Setup dialog box. To get there, go to the Page Layout tab and click the Page Setup dialog launcher. Once the Page Setup dialog box activates, you can click on the Sheet tab. There, you can set the Print Area input to the cell range you want to print. ■

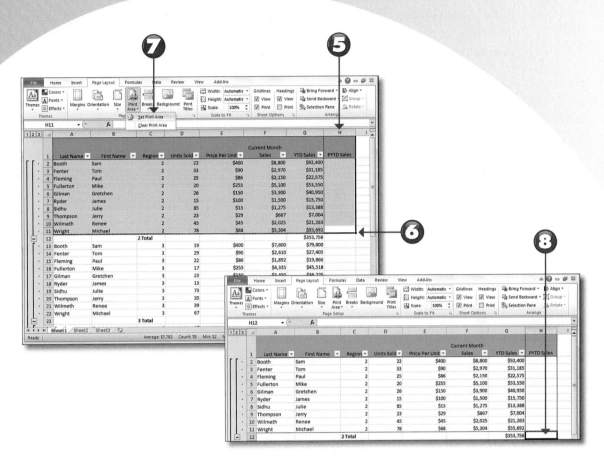

5 Insert a row or column into your worksheet (PYTD Sales, for example). Parts of the table now fall outside the current print area.

6 Select the exact cells you want to print (now including the extra column).

7 To reset the print area to include the new row or column, choose **Print Area** from the Page Layout Tab, and select **Set Print Area**.

8 Your new print area is stored as part of this worksheet. If the new print area falls outside the margins, see the next task.

End

NOTE

Long and Short Dashes   The long dashed lines in your worksheet indicate the print area, and the smaller dashed lines indicate the current page margins. If your print area data falls outside the current page margins, you need to alter the page margins. ◼

ADJUSTING PAGE MARGINS

Margins affect where data is printed on a page. They also determine where headers and footers are printed. Occasionally, margins might need to be changed to make room for a letterhead or logo on preprinted stationery. When in Print Preview mode, Excel enables you to simultaneously alter your column widths and margins.

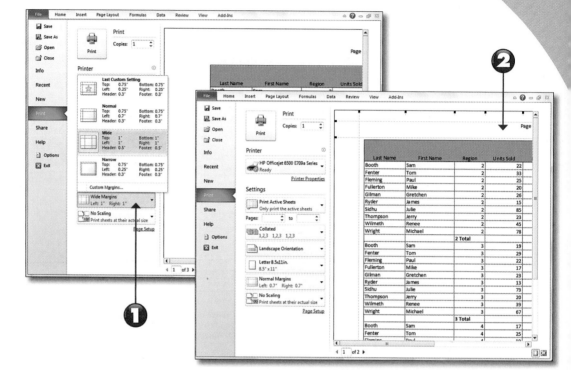

Start

1 When in Print Preview mode, if you have a page that displays some carryover data from another page, click the **Margins** button. You can select from one of the default margin settings or customize.

2 Excel activates Print Preview's margin lines. Press **page up** or **page down** to display the page in your worksheet on which you want to fit all the data.

Continued

NOTE

Entering Specific Margins If you need to enter specific margin measurements, the Page Setup dialog box is a better option. Go to the Page Layout tab and click the Page Setup dialog launcher. Once the Page Setup dialog box activates, you can click on the Margins tab and alter the margins as necessary (Left, Right, Top, Bottom, Header, Footer). Click the OK button to return to your worksheet or Print to print immediately. ■

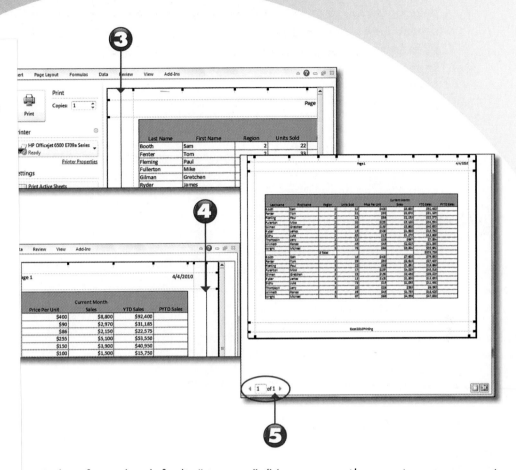

argin line from the default 1" to 0.34". (You can see the exact measurement ft corner of the screen.)

ne **Right Margin** line from the default 1" to 0.34". (Again, you can see the ent in the bottom-left corner of the screen.)

argin change, the total number of pages to print is reduced.

End

INSERTING PAGE BREAKS

When a worksheet page is filled to the margins with data, Excel automatically inserts a page break for you. There may be times, however, when you want to manually insert a page break. For example, if you create a report with multiple topic sections, you might want each topic to begin on a new page. Inserting a page break enables you to print each page separately. The best way to insert page breaks is using Page Break Preview view (instead of Normal view).

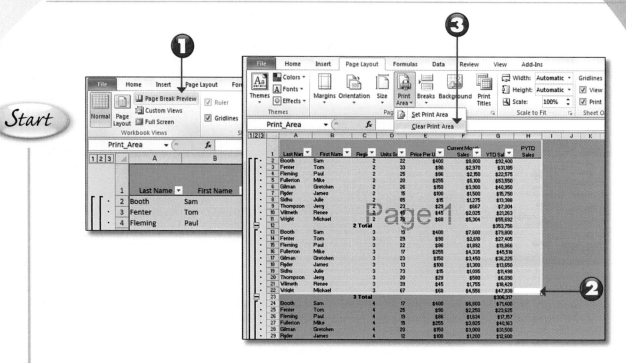

① Open the View tab and choose **Page Break Preview** to change to Page Break Preview mode.

② Press the page up and page down keys on the keyboard to move through your worksheet in Page Break Preview. Notice that cells outside the print area are grayed out.

③ Open the Page Layout tab, choose Print Area, and select **Clear Print Area** to eliminate any current print area settings.

Continued

NOTE

Removing Page Breaks To remove a page break, place the active cell so that one of the cell borders is touching the page break line. Then, select the Page Layout tab and choose Remove Page Break. (You can also do this in Normal view.) ■

NOTE

Page Break Intersection A page break is always inserted as an intersection between rows and columns. If the active cell isn't in the first column, the page break will be inserted as four quadrants. ■

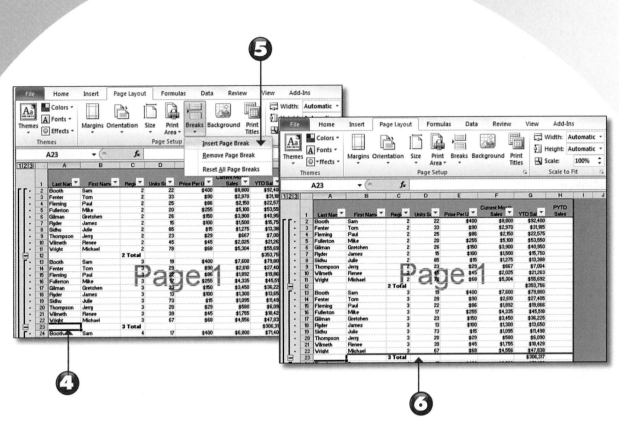

4 Click the cell below and in the left-most column in which you want to insert a page break.

5 On the Page Layout tab choose Breaks, **Insert Page Break** to insert the page break.

6 The page break is inserted.

End

TIP

Why Not Simply Add More Rows Suppose you want each of two tables that fit on one page to print on separate pages. Instead of inserting a page break, you could add several blank rows to the end of the first table, which automatically kicks the second one onto a second page. If, however, you later add any rows to the first table and forget to delete the same number of blank rows before the second one, the tables might not print correctly. ■

WORKING IN PAGE BREAK PREVIEW MODE

Page Break Preview mode displays the area you have selected for your set print area. It also enables you to click and drag where your page breaks are instead of using the Insert, Page Break command. You can also edit the text and data just as you can in Normal view.

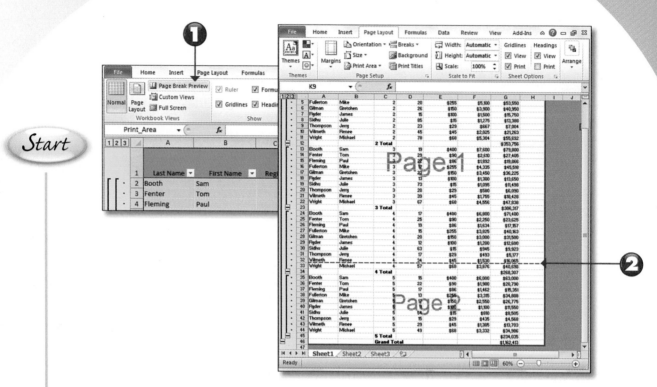

Start

1 Click **Page Break Preview** from the View tab on the ribbon. If a print area has been set, it is displayed; if not, the entire worksheet is displayed.

2 Move through the worksheet to find page breaks (if any). Naturally occurring page breaks appear as blue dashed lines, and inserted page breaks appear as solid blue lines.

Continued

NOTE

Clearing the Print Area If you need to set only the print area to print a portion of data in your worksheet once, you probably want to clear the print area after you print. Go to the Page Layout tab, click the Print Area command, and select Clear Print Area. ■

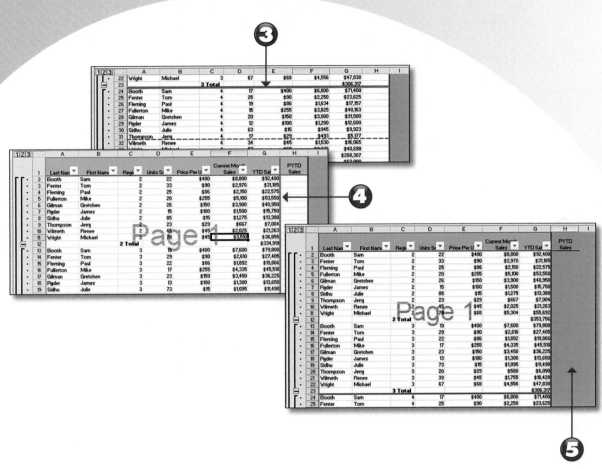

3 To move a page break that is poorly placed, click and drag it to a better location. (Moving a natural page break changes it to an inserted break—solid-blue.)

4 To exclude a column or data to the right of your set print area, click and drag the vertical page break.

5 The excluded column outside the print area is grayed out.

End

TIP

Removing a Page Break To remove a page break in Page Break Preview mode, click and drag the page break line off to the right/left/top/bottom of the worksheet. ■

PRINTING A WORKSHEET ON ONE PAGE

By default, Excel prints your worksheet at a scale of 100%. You can decrease this percentage if you want to fit more data on a page, or increase it to fit less data on a page. In addition, you can have Excel fit your entire worksheet on one page. (If your worksheet is large, the data might become too tiny to read when scaled down.)

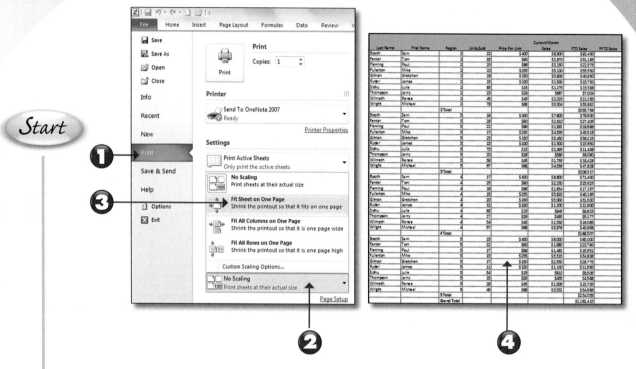

Start

1 Go the **File** tab and click **Print**.

2 Click the **Zoom and Scaling** drop-down.

3 Select the **Fit Sheet on One Page** option.

4 Your worksheet appears in Print Preview mode, all on one page.

End

TIP

Changing from Letter to Legal   To choose a different paper size for your printout, click the Paper Size dropdown on the Print pane of the Backstage View. There, you can select Legal. The scaling setting automatically adjusts to the selected paper size. ■

NOTE

Returning to the Default Scale   When you want to return the preview of your worksheet to the default scale, return the Scaling dropdown to the No Scaling option. ■

PRINTING IN PORTRAIT OR LANDSCAPE ORIENTATION

Not all Excel reports are the same. Some reports have just a few columns, while others are very wide with many columns. Depending on your report, you will either print in Portrait or Landscape orientation. The default orientation in Excel is Portrait, meaning the report can fit vertically on one page without the sides being cut off. Landscape orientation means that your page is printed horizontally (on its side) so that you get that extra room on the sides for more columns to fit.

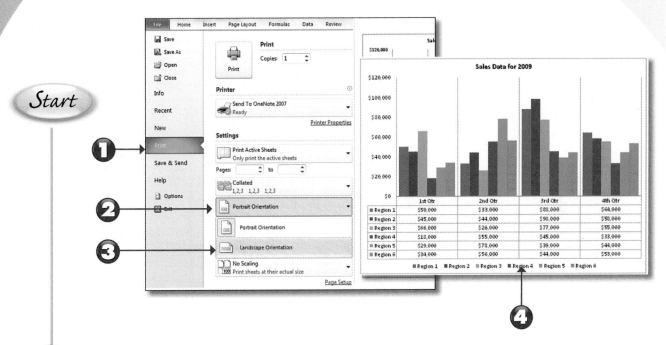

Start

1 Go the **File** tab and click **Print**.

2 Click the **Orientation** drop-down.

3 Select the **Landscape Orientation** option.

4 Your report is now in Landscape orientation.

End

CENTERING A WORKSHEET ON A PAGE

If you want a cleaner, more professional looking printout for a presentation, you might want to center your worksheet data on the page before you print it. This is a particularly good idea if you plan to print your worksheet on one page.

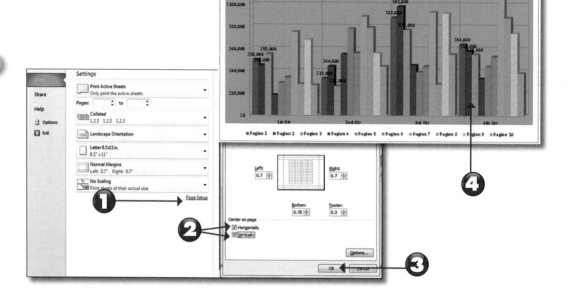

Go to the Print pane in the Backstage View and click the **Page Setup** link.

On the Margins tab, click the **Horizontally** and/or **Vertically** check boxes in the Center on page area.

Click **OK**.

Your worksheet appears in Print Preview mode, centered.

End

TIP

Centering Vertically or Horizontally   You don't have to center your data both vertically and horizontally. You can choose one or the other, depending on how you want your printed worksheet to look. ■

PRINTING GRIDLINES AND ROW/COLUMN HEADERS

By default, Excel doesn't print worksheet gridlines or row/column headers. You can, however, instruct Excel to print them. Gridlines help you read information in a printed worksheet, keeping rows and columns of data visually organized. Row and column headers can help you quickly find data in your worksheet.

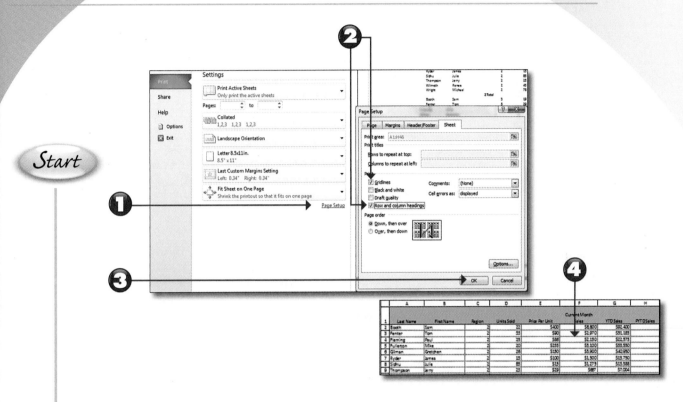

Start

1. Go to the Print pane in the Backstage View and click the **Page Setup** link.

2. On the Sheet tab, click the **Gridlines** and **Row** and column headings check boxes in the Print area to select them.

3. Click **OK**.

4. Your worksheet appears in Print Preview mode with gridlines and row/column headers visible.

End

NOTE

Repeating Titles   Displaying row and column headers is not the same as printing repeating titles. Repeating titles are column headers and row headers that you have assigned in your worksheet. For more information, see the task "Printing Repeating Row and Column Titles" later in this chapter. ∎

PRINTING CELL COMMENTS

Some cells contain data or formulas that require an explanation or special attention. Comments provide a way to attach this type of information to individual cells. A red triangle in the upper-right corner of the cell indicates that a comment is present. Check Chapter 3, "Entering and Managing Data," for more information on using comments.

This task shows you how to print your worksheets so that the printouts include the information in your comments, either as they appear in the worksheet or at the end of the worksheet.

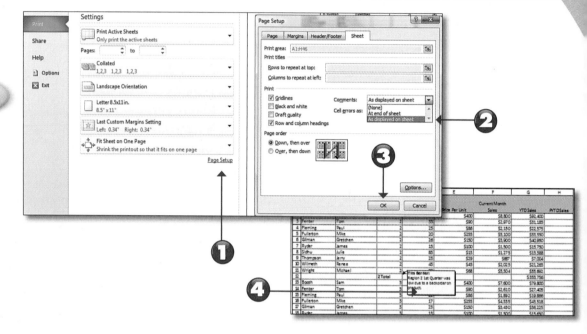

1 Go to the Print pane in the Backstage View and click the **Page Setup** link.

2 On the Sheet tab, click the **Comments** field down arrow and choose either **At End of Sheet**, to print the comments, **As Displayed on Sheet**, or (**None**).

3 Click **OK**.

4 View your worksheet in Print Preview mode to review the comments as displayed in your worksheet (as in this example) or at the end of your worksheet.

End

NOTE

As Displayed on Sheet You must have your comments "showing" in your worksheet (choose View, Comments) for them to display when the As Displayed on Sheet Option is selected. If they aren't showing, they won't display in the printout or in Print Preview.

PRINTING CELL ERROR INDICATORS

When you print worksheets for friends or colleagues (or even yourself), calculation errors that appear on your worksheet can create a negative impression, which is why they're not printed by default. If you want these errors to be visible in your printout, however, you can display them or replace them with any of the following: <blank>, --, or #N/A.

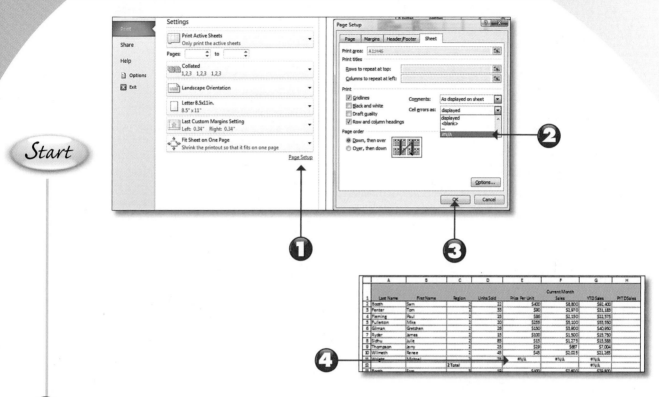

Start

1 Go to the Print pane in the Backstage View and click the **Page Setup** link.

2 On the Sheet tab, click the down arrow next to the Cell errors as field and choose displayed, <blank>, --, or #N/A depending on how you want errors to be displayed.

3 Click **OK**.

4 View your worksheet in Print Preview mode to review how cells containing errors display.

End

NOTE

Errors That Print All the error messages explained in Chapter 5, "Working with Formulas and Functions," (#DIV/o!, #Name?, #Value!, #REF!, and Circular Reference errors) will print.

PRINTING REPEATING ROW AND COLUMN TITLES

You might have noticed that when a worksheet spans multiple pages, it is difficult to keep the column and row titles organized. A quick way to rectify this is to make particular titles repeat on each page of the printed worksheet.

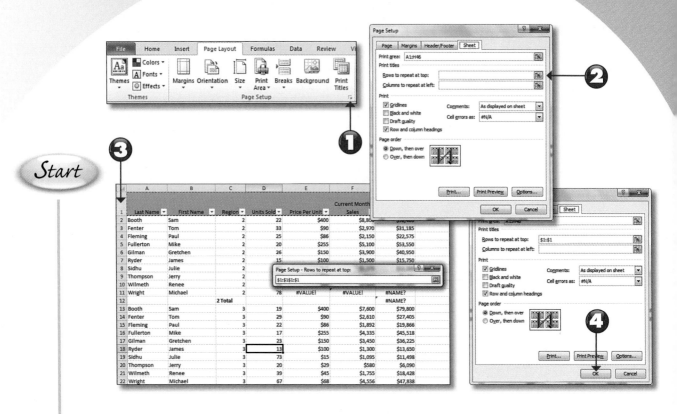

Start

1. Go to the Page Layout tab and click the **Page Setup** dialog launcher.

2. Click the **Rows to repeat at top** selection box in the Print titles area. Excel shrinks the Page Setup dialog box, making your focus the worksheet on your desktop.

3. Click the row containing the titles that you want to repeat on each page of your worksheet, and press **Enter** to reopen the Page Setup dialog box with your selection inserted.

4. Click **OK**. If you want, view the worksheet in Print Preview mode to get an idea of what your printed worksheet will look like with repeating row headings.

End

NOTE

Repeating Column Headings To repeat column headings across several pages, follow the steps in this task, but click the Columns to repeat at the left selection box in step 2. Then, click the columns you want to repeat, and proceed as normal.

ADDING HEADERS AND FOOTERS

Headers and footers appear at the top and bottom of printed pages of Excel worksheets and can display the filename, the date and time the worksheet was printed, and the worksheet's name, or you can create your own custom header or footer.

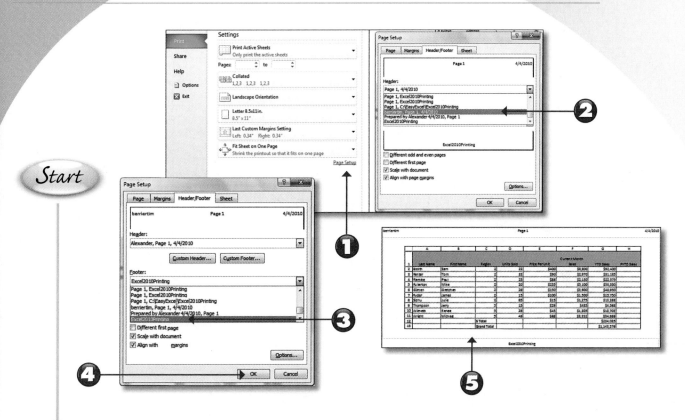

Start

1 Go to the Print pane in the Backstage View and click the **Page Setup** link.

2 On the Header/Footer tab, click the down arrow next to the Header field, and scroll through the header options. If you see one you like, click it to see what it looks like.

3 Click the down arrow next to the Footer, and scroll through the footer options. If you see one you like, click it to see what it looks like.

4 Click **OK**.

5 You can view the worksheet in Print Preview mode to get an idea of what your printed worksheet will look like with headers and footers.

End

PRINTING WORKSHEETS

Printing a worksheet, workbook, or chart sheet is quite simple, but setting the options for printing can be complex. The number of options that must be set before printing depends on the amount of data stored in the workbook, how it is arranged, how much of it needs to be printed, and how you want the printout to look.

Start

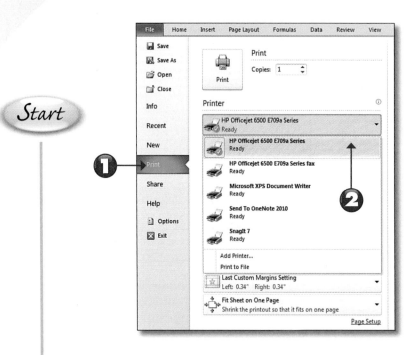

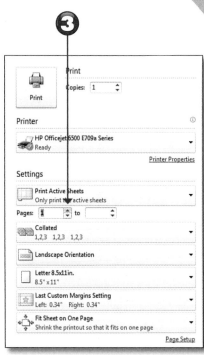

① Go the File tab and click **Print**.

② Click the down arrow next to the Printer Name field to choose the printer or fax you want to use.

③ In the Print range area, click **Page(s) From and To**, and type the pages you want to include in the range (for example, from 2 to 5) or keep the All (default).

Continued

NOTE

Vertical or Horizontal Page Order   If you work with a large worksheet, you can specify the page order for your worksheet. Go to the Page Layout tab and click the Page Setup dialog launcher. Once the Page Setup dialog box activates, you can click on the Sheet tab. Review the options of Down, then over (default) and Over, and then down in the Page order area of the Page Setup dialog box. ■

NOTE

Setting Additional Print Options   To set additional print options, such as the paper size, graphic options, font options, and printer details, click the Printer Properties link in the Print section of Backstage view. ■

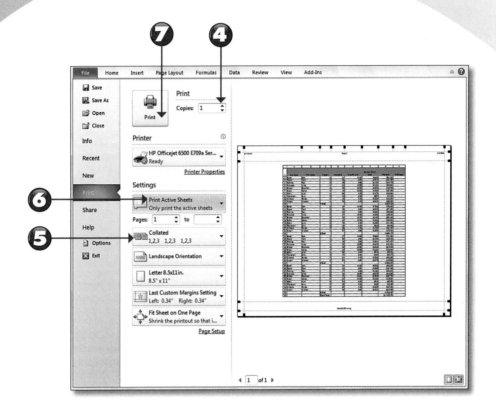

4 Type the number of copies you want to print in the Number of Copies field, which defaults to 1.

5 If you want the printed pages to be collated, click the **Collate** drop-down to set that option.

6 In the Settings group, click either Selection (only selected cells), Active Sheet(s) (currently sheets), or Entire workbook (all worksheets and chart sheets).

7 Click the **Print** button to send your printout to the printer.

End

TIP

Quick Printing You can add the Quick Print command to your Quick Access Toolbar. This allows you to print your entire worksheet without going to the Backstage View. But Revisit Chapter 1 "Working with the Excel User Interface" for a refresher on how to add commands to the Quick Access Toolbar. ∎

Chapter 9

WORKING WITH EXCEL PIVOT TABLES

A pivot table is an analysis tool that allows you to create an interactive view of your dataset. We call this view a pivot table report. With a pivot table report, you can quickly and easily categorize your data into groups, summarize large amounts of data into meaningful information, and perform a wide variety of calculations in a fraction of the time it takes by hand. But the real power of a pivot table report is that you can interactively drag and drop fields within your report, dynamically changing your perspective and recalculating totals to fit your current view.

A pivot table is composed of four areas, the Values area, the Row Area, the Column Area, and the Filter Area. The values area is the area that calculates and counts data. The data fields that you drag and drop here are typically those that you want to measure, such as Sum of Revenue, Count of Units, or Average of Price.

The row area displays the unique field values down the rows of the left side of the pivot table. The row area typically has at least one field, although it's possible to have no fields. The types of data fields that you would drop here include those that you want to group and categorize, such as, Products, Names, and Locations.

The column area displays the unique field values across the top of the pivot table. The column area is ideal for creating a data matrix or showing trends over time.

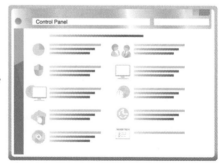

The filter area is an optional set of one or more drop-downs at the top of the pivot table. Placing data fields into the filter area allows you to filter the entire pivot table based on your selections. The types of data fields that you'd drop here include those that you want to isolate and focus on; for example, Region, Line of Business, and Employees.

THE ANATOMY OF A PIVOT TABLE

Filter Area

Column Area

Row Area

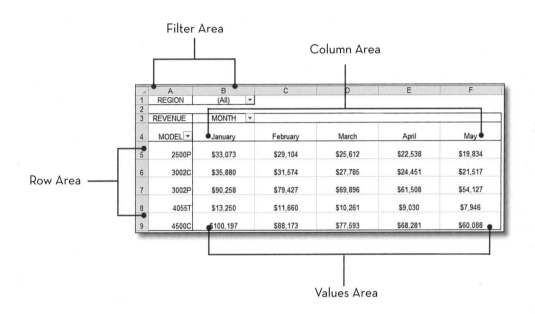

Values Area

CREATING A PIVOT TABLE

Before you create a pivot table, you should ask yourself two questions; "What am I measuring?" and "How do I want to see it?" The answer to these questions gives you some guidance when determining which areas you will place your data fields.

In this scenario, we want to see dollar sales by market. This means we need a Sales field and a Market field. How do you want to see that? We want markets to go down the left side of the report and dollar sales to be calculated next to each market.

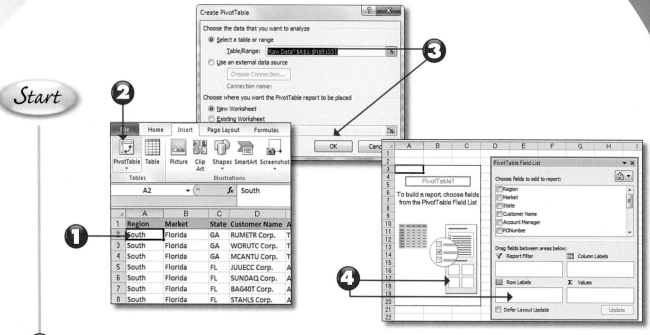

Click any single cell inside your data table.

Select the **Insert** tab in the Ribbon, and then click the **PivotTable** command.

This activates the Create PivotTable dialog box. Specify the location of your source data, and then click the **OK** button.

Observe that you have an empty pivot table report on a new worksheet. Next to the pivot table, you will see the PivotTable Field List.

Continued

NOTE

Pivot Table Default Location Note that in the Create PivotTable dialog box, the default location for a new pivot table is New Worksheet. You can change this by selecting the Existing Worksheet option and specifying the worksheet where you want the pivot table placed. ■

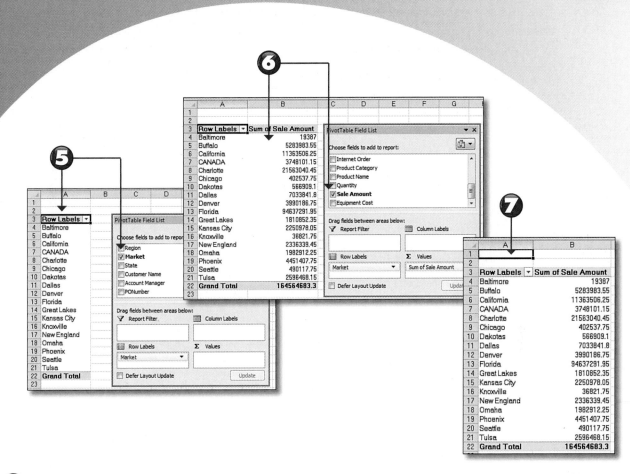

 Find the **Market** field in field selector and place a check next to it. Note that the Market field is automatically placed in the Row area of the pivot table.

 Scroll down the PivotTable Field List and find the **Sales Amount** field. Place a check next to it and note the Sales Amount field is automatically placed in the Values area.

Click off your pivot table to make the PivotTable Field List disappear. Observe your first pivot table.

End

NOTE

How Excel Knows where to Place Data   Placing a check next to any field that is non-numeric (text or date) automatically places that field into the row area of the pivot table. Placing a check next to any field that is numeric automatically places that field in the values area of the pivot table. ■

TIP

Activating the PivotTable Field List   The PivotTable Field List typically activates when you click anywhere on your pivot table. If clicking the pivot table doesn't activate the PivotTable Field List dialog box, you can manually activate it by right-clicking anywhere inside the pivot table and selecting Show Field List. ■

REARRANGING A PIVOT TABLE

The nifty thing about pivot tables is that you can add as many layers of analysis as made possible by the fields in your source data table. For instance, if we wanted to show the dollar sales each market earned by product category, we could simply drag the Product Category field to the Column area.

Start

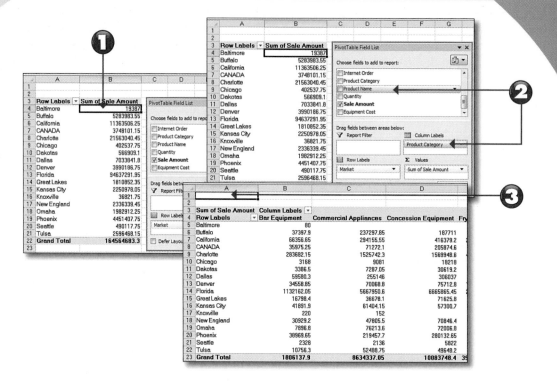

① Click anywhere on your pivot table to reactivate the PivotTable Field List.

② Find the **Product Category** field, click it and drag it to the Column area in the Pivot Table Field List.

③ Click off your pivot table to make the PivotTable Field List disappear, and note how your pivot table now shows a matrix style view.

End

TIP

Dragging Fields from One Area to Another You're not limited to only dragging fields from the field list. You can drag fields from one area to another. For example, you can drag the product category field from the column area to the row area. This is a fairly powerful benefit in that it lets you experiment with the look and feel of your pivot table reports. ■

REFRESHING PIVOT TABLE DATA

When you create a pivot table, Excel takes a snapshot of your data source and stores it in a pivot cache. A pivot cache is a special memory container. This is what your pivot table is connected to. This means that your pivot table report and your data source are disconnected.

The benefit of this is optimization. Any changes you make to the pivot table report, such as rearranging fields, adding new fields, or hiding items, are made rapidly and with minimal overhead. However, because your pivot table is working from a snapshot of your data source, any changes you make to your data are not picked up by your pivot table report until you take another snapshot. This is called "refreshing" your pivot table.

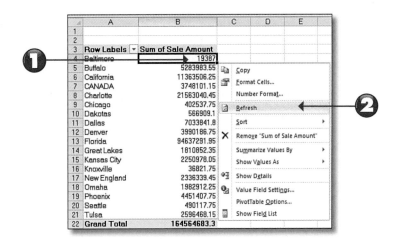

1 Right-click anywhere in your pivot table.

2 Select the **Refresh** option.

End

NOTE

The PivotTable Tools Contextual Tab When you click on your pivot table, Excel activates the PivotTable Tools contextual tab. There, you see an Options tab and a Design tab. Click the Options tab and choose the Refresh command. These tabs expose a variety of commands you can use to manage and work with pivot tables. ■

ADDING A REPORT FILTER

Often times, you're asked to produce reports for one particular region, market, product, and so on. Instead of working hours and hours building separate reports for every possible analysis scenario, you can leverage pivot tables to help create multiple views of the same data. For example, you can do so by creating a region filter in your pivot table.

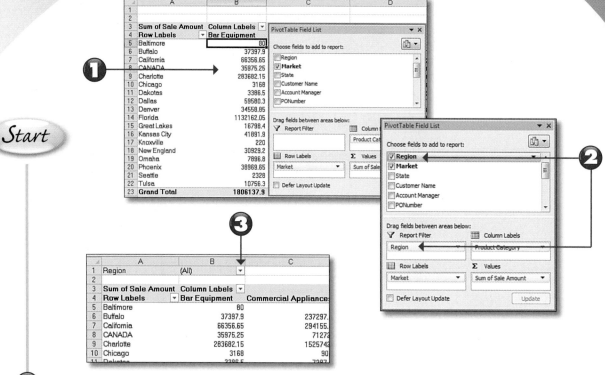

 Start

1 Click anywhere on your pivot table to reactivate the PivotTable Field List.

2 Find the **Region** field, click it and drag it to the Report Filter area in the Pivot Table Field List.

3 Note that your pivot table now has a filter drop-down for Region.

Continued

TIP

Using a Field's Context Menu to Move It In addition to dragging, you can also move a field into the different areas of the pivot table by clicking the black triangle next to the field name and then selecting the desired area. ■

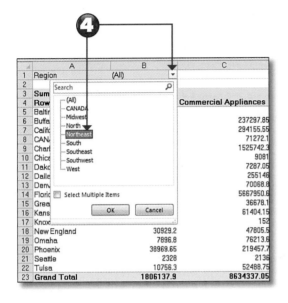

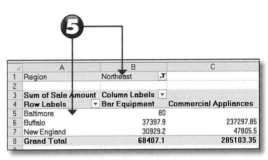

④ Once you have a report filter on your pivot table, you can click the filter drop-down and select the desired data item.

⑤ Note how the pivot table responds by showing you only the data for the selected item.

End

TIP

Selecting Multiple Data Items When you click the filter drop-down to select a data item, you will notice a check box labeled **Select Multiple Items**. Clicking this check box allows you to select more than one data item by which you can filter your report. ■

ADDING PIVOT TABLE DATA

Sometimes, the data source that feeds your pivot table changes in structure. For example, you may have added or deleted rows or columns from your data table. These types of changes affect the range of your data source, not just a few data items in the table. In these cases, performing a simple Refresh of your pivot table won't do. You have to update the range being captured by the pivot table.

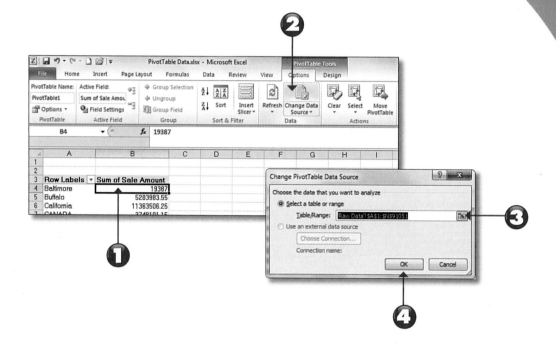

① Click anywhere in your pivot table to activate the PivotTable Tools contextual tab.

② Select the **Change Data Source** command in the Options tab.

③ The Change PivotTable Data Source dialog box activates. Here, you supply the new data range for the pivot table.

④ Click the **OK** button to confirm the change. Your pivot table automatically refreshes to show the newly referenced data.

End

CHANGING THE PIVOT TABLE LAYOUT

Excel 2010 gives you a choice of three layouts for your pivot tables. The three layouts are the Compact Form, Outline Form, and Tabular Form. Although no layout stands out as being better than the others, the most popular layout is, by far, the Tabular Form. This is mainly because the tabular layout was the one that existed in previous versions of Excel, so most people who have seen pivot tables in the past are used to that layout.

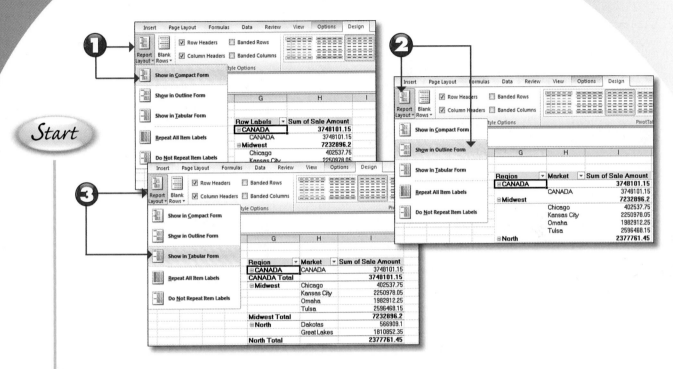

1 Show your pivot table in the **Compact** layout. Go to the Design tab, click on the **Report Layout** drop-down and select **Show in Compact Form**.

2 Show your pivot table in **Outline** layout. Go to the Design tab, click on the **Report Layout** drop-down and select **Show in Outline Form**.

3 Show your pivot table in **Tabular** layout. Go to the Design tab, click on the **Report Layout** drop-down and select **Show in Tabular Form**.

End

CUSTOMIZING FIELD NAMES

Notice that every field in your pivot table has a name. The fields in the row, column, and filter areas inherit their names from the data labels in your source table. The fields in the Values area are given a name, such as Sum of Sales Amount. There will often be times when you might prefer another name for your fields. For instance, you may want your Value field called Total Sales instead of Sum of Sales Amount.

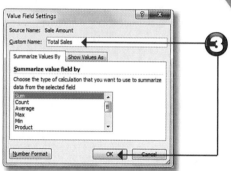

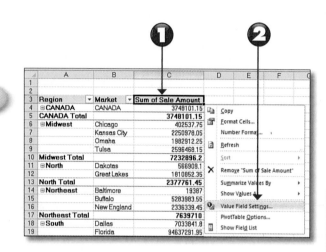

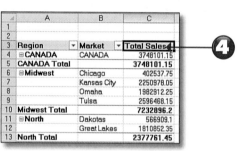

Start

1 Right-click the field **Sum of Sales Amount**.

2 Select **Value Field Settings**.

3 Enter the new name in the Custom Name input box and click **OK** to confirm.

4 Note that the name of your pivot field changed.

End

NOTE

Pivot Field Naming Restriction   You cannot rename a pivot field to the same name used in your source table. To get around this, you can name the field and add a space to the end of the name. For example, Excel considers Sales Amount (followed by a space) to be different from Sales Amount. This way you can use the name you want, and no one will notice it's any different. ∎

APPLYING NUMERIC FORMATS TO DATA FIELDS

Numbers in pivot tables can be formatted to fit your needs (that is, formatted as currency, percentage, or number). You can easily control the numeric formatting of a field using the Value Field Settings dialog box.

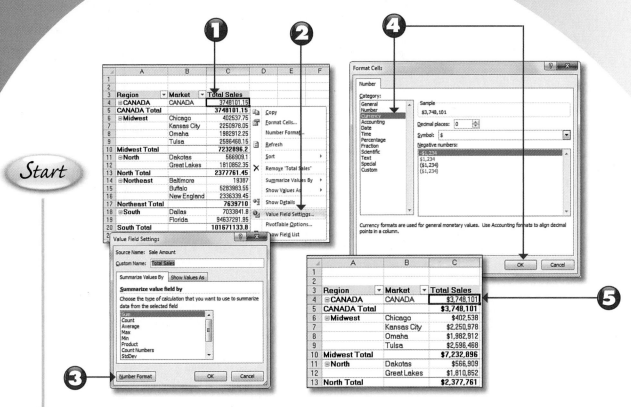

Start

End

① Right-click any value within the target field. For example, if you want to change the format of the values in the Sales Amount field, right-click any value under that field.

② Select **Value Field Settings**.

③ The Value Field Settings dialog box appears. Click the **Number Format** button.

④ The Format Cells dialog box activates. Apply the number format you desire, just as you normally would on your spreadsheet. Click **OK** to apply the changes.

⑤ After you set the formatting for a field, the applied formatting will persist even if you refresh or rearrange your pivot table.

TIP

Getting to Field Settings from the Ribbon You can also get to the Value Field Settings dialog box via the Ribbon. Click the Field Settings command under the Options tab. ■

CHANGING SUMMARY CALCULATIONS

When creating your pivot table report, Excel will, by default, summarize your data by either counting or summing the items. Instead of Sum or Count, you might want to choose functions, such as Average, Min, Max, and so on. You can easily change the summary calculation for any given field by following these steps.

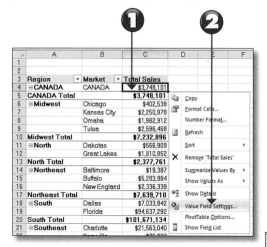

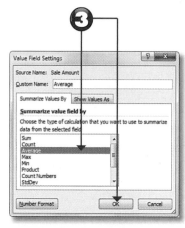

Start

1 Right-click any value within the target field.

2 Select **Value Field Settings**.

3 The Value Field Settings dialog box appears. Choose the type of calculation you want to use from the list of calculations, then click **OK** to confirm.

4 Note that the pivot table now shows your chosen calculation.

End

NOTE

How Excel Chooses Sum or Count   When you click on a numeric field in the PivotTable Field List, Excel automatically places that field in the Values area. However, Excel doesn't necessarily apply a Sum to that field. If all the cells in a column contain numeric data, Excel chooses a Sum calculation by default. However, if just one cell in that same column is either blank or contains text, Excel chooses the Count calculation. ■

SHOWING AND HIDING DATA ITEMS

A pivot table summarizes and displays all the records in your source data table. There may, however, be situations when you want to inhibit certain data items from being included in your pivot table summary. In these situations, you can choose to hide a data item. In terms of pivot tables, hiding doesn't just mean preventing the data item from being shown on the report, hiding a data item also prevents it from being factored into the summary calculations. For example, you can hide the Canada market to see only sales for U.S. markets.

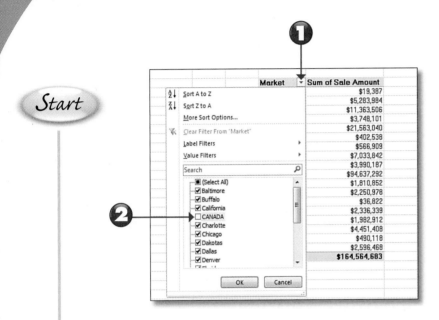

Start

1. Click on the drop-down for the field you are filtering—in this case, the Market field.

2. Remove the check from the data item you want hidden. Here, Canada is being removed so that only U.S. sales are calculated.

3. After the filter has been applied, you'll note that not only is the Canada market hidden, but the grand total has recalculated to show the total of U.S. markets only.

End

TIP

Clear Applied Filters   To return a pivot field to its normal unfiltered state, right click on any value for that field and select Filter -> Clear Filter from [field name]. To clear all the filters in the pivot table at one time, go to the Options tab, click the Clear command, and then click Clear All. ■

SORTING YOUR PIVOT TABLE

By default, items in each pivot field are sorted in ascending sequence based on the item name. Excel gives you the freedom to change the sort order of the items in your pivot table. Like many actions you can perform in Excel, there are dozens of different ways to sort data within a pivot table. The easiest way is to apply the sort directly in the pivot table.

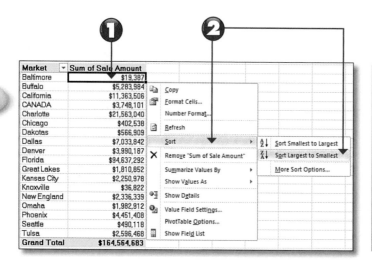

Start

1 Right-click any value within the target field.

2 Select Sort followed by the sort direction. In this case, the data is sorted on Sales Amount with the largest numbers at the top.

3 Note that the pivot table now sorts the values per your instructions.

End

NOTE

Sorting Persists in a Pivot Table   When you sort data in a standard worksheet, it's really a one-time event. That is to say, if you add data to your data table after sorting, you will need to sort again. In a pivot table, however, the sorting persists. If new data is introduced to a sorted pivot table, the new value is automatically sorted and based on the sort rules you implement. There is no need to reapply the sort. ■

EXCEL SHORTCUT KEYS

Throughout this book, I've introduced you to a host of Excel shortcut keys. As you have learned, Excel shortcut keys allow you to perform certain tasks using only the keyboard, which limits the number of instances your hands have to move back and forth from the keyboard to the mouse thereby saving you precious time. Getting in the habit of using these shortcut keys can help you work more efficiently and become more productive.

USING THE EXCEL SHORTCUT KEY REFERENCE TABLE

The table included here lists the keyboard shortcuts I have covered during this book, and many more that you have not yet seen. You can use this appendix as an ongoing reference of the more commonly used Excel shortcut keys.

The **Key** column lists the root key on the keyboard you need to press. The **Alone** column tells you what task is triggered if the root key is pressed by itself. Some keys like the F1 key trigger a task when pressed alone, while others (like the letter A) do not cause Excel to take any action.

The **Shift** column tells you what task is triggered if the root key is pressed with the Shift key. For example the F5 key pressed in conjunction with the Shift key (Shift+F5) activates the Find dialog box.

The **Ctrl** column tells you what task is triggered if the root key is pressed with the Ctrl key. For example the B key pressed in conjunction with the Ctrl key (Ctrl+B) applies the Bold font to selected text.

The **Alt** column tells you what task is triggered if the root key is pressed with the Alt key. For example the F4 key pressed in conjunction with the Alt key (Alt+F4) closes Excel.

The **Ctrl+Shift** column tells you what task is triggered if the root key is pressed with the Ctrl and the Shift keys together. For example the F12 key pressed in conjunction with the Ctrl and Shift keys (Ctrl+Shift+F12) prints the active workbook.

EXCEL SHORTCUT KEYS

Key	Alone	Shift	Ctrl	Alt	Ctrl+Shift
F1	Help	What's This Help	—	Insert Chart Sheet	—
F2	Edit Mode	Edit Comment	—	Save As	—
F3	Paste Name Formula	Paste Function	Define Name	—	Names From Labels
F4	Repeat Action	Find Again	Close Window	Quit Excel	—
F5	Goto	Find	Restore Window Size	—	—
F6	Next Pane	Prev Pane	Next Workbook	Switch To VBA	Prev Workbook
F7	Spell Check	—	Move Window	—	—
F8	Extend Selection	Add To Selection	Resize Window	Macro List	—
F9	Calculate All	Calculate Worksheet	Minimize Workbook	—	—
F10	Activate Menu	Context Menu	Restore Workbook	—	—
F11	New Chart	New Worksheet	New Macro Sheet	VB Editor	—
F12	Save As	Save	Open	—	Print
A	—	—	Select All	—	Formula Arguments
B	—	—	Bold	—	—
C	—	—	Copy	—	—
D	—	—	Fill Down	Data Menu	—
E	—	—	—	Edit Menu	—
F	—	—	Find	File Menu	Font Name
G	—	—	Goto	—	—
H	—	—	Replace	Help Menu	—
I	—	—	Italics	Insert Menu	—
J	—	—	—	—	—
K	—	—	Insert Hyperlink	—	—
L	—	—	—	—	—
M	—	—	—	—	—
N	—	—	New Workbook	—	—

Key	Alone	Shift	Ctrl	Alt	Ctrl+Shift
O	–	–	Open Workbook	Format Menu	Select Comments
P	–	–	Print	–	Font Size
Q	–	–	–	–	–
R	–	–	Fill Right	–	–
S	–	–	Save	–	–
T	–	–	–	Tools Menu	–
U	–	–	Underline	–	–
V	–	–	Paste	–	–
W	–	–	Close Workbook	Window Menu	–
X	–	–	Cut	–	–
Y	–	–	Repeat Active	–	–
Z	–	–	Undo	–	–
~	–	–	Toggle Formula View	–	General Format
!	–	–	Cell Format	–	Number Format
@	–	–	Toggle Bold	–	Time Format
#	–	–	Toggle Italics	–	Date Format
$	–	–	Toggle Underline	–	Currency Format
%	–	–	Toggle Strikethru	–	Percent Format
^	–	–	–	–	Exponent Format
&	–	–	–	–	Apply Border
*	–	–	Outline	–	Select Region
(	–	–	Hide Rows	–	Unhide Rows
)	–	–	Hide Columns	–	Unhide Columns
-	–	–	Delete Selection	Control Menu	No Border
+	Formula	–	–	Auto Sum	Insert dialog

Key	Alone	Shift	Ctrl	Alt	Ctrl+Shift
;	—	—	Insert Date	Select Visible Cells	Insert Time
'	—	—	—	Style	Copy Cell Value Above
:	—	—	Insert Time	—	—
/	—	—	Select Array	—	Select Array
\	—	—	Select Differences	—	Select Unequal Cells
Insert	Insert Mode	—	Copy	—	—
Delete	Clear	—	Delete To End Of Line	—	—
Home	Begin Row	—	Start Of Worksheet	—	—
End	End Row	—	End Of Worksheet	—	—
Page Up	Page Up	—	Previous Worksheet	Left 1 screen	—
Page Down	Page Down	—	Next Worksheet	Right 1 screen	Select Down
Left Arrow	Move Left	Select Left	Move Left Area	—	Select Left
Right Arrow	Move Right	Select Right	Move Right Area	—	Select Right
Up Arrow	Move Up	Select Up	Move Up Area	—	Select Up
Down Arrow	Move Down	Select Down	Move Down Area	Drop down list	Select Down
Space Bar	Space	Select Row	Select Column	Control Box	Select Entire Used Range
Tab	Move Right	Move Left	Next Window	Next Application	Previous Window

Index

Symbols

D

informit.com/register

Register the Addison-Wesley, Exam Cram, Prentice Hall, Que, and Sams products you own to unlock great benefits.

To begin the registration process, simply go to **informit.com/register** to sign in or create an account. You will then be prompted to enter the 10- or 13-digit ISBN that appears on the back cover of your product.

Registering your products can unlock the following benefits:

- Access to supplemental content, including bonus chapters, source code, or project files.
- A coupon to be used on your next purchase.

Registration benefits vary by product. Benefits will be listed on your Account page under Registered Products.

About InformIT — THE TRUSTED TECHNOLOGY LEARNING SOURCE

INFORMIT IS HOME TO THE LEADING TECHNOLOGY PUBLISHING IMPRINTS Addison-Wesley Professional, Cisco Press, Exam Cram, IBM Press, Prentice Hall Professional, Que, and Sams. Here you will gain access to quality and trusted content and resources from the authors, creators, innovators, and leaders of technology. Whether you're looking for a book on a new technology, a helpful article, timely newsletters, or access to the Safari Books Online digital library, InformIT has a solution for you.

informIT.com

THE TRUSTED TECHNOLOGY LEARNING SOURCE

Addison-Wesley | Cisco Press | Exam Cram
IBM Press | Que | Prentice Hall | Sams

SAFARI BOOKS ONLINE

FREE Online Edition

Your purchase of **Easy Microsoft® Excel® 2010** includes access to a free online edition for 45 days through the Safari Books Online subscription service. Nearly every Que book is available online through Safari Books Online, along with more than 5,000 other technical books and videos from publishers such as Addison-Wesley Professional, Cisco Press, Exam Cram, IBM Press, O'Reilly, Prentice Hall, and Sams.

SAFARI BOOKS ONLINE allows you to search for a specific answer, cut and paste code, download chapters, and stay current with emerging technologies.

Activate your FREE Online Edition at
www.informit.com/safarifree

> **STEP 1:** Enter the coupon code: MKYEHBI.

> **STEP 2:** New Safari users, complete the brief registration form.
> Safari subscribers, just log in.

If you have difficulty registering on Safari or accessing the online edition, please e-mail customer-service@safaribooksonline.com